ADAPTING ELSEWHERE

A PRACTICAL GUIDE FOR AMERICANS MOVING ABROAD

SCOTT SCHWARTZ

KODA
PUBLISHING

Library of Congress Control Number: 2026908910

ISBN: 978-1-7373329-2-3

Contributor: Tom Zachystal

Cover and book design: Jill Turney Design

Cover photos:
Paris Skyline © StockByM | iStock
Valetta, Malta © javarman3 | iStock
Map of Europe © Nellmac | iStock

Table of Contents

FOREWORD

When Scott first shared the concept for Adapting Elsewhere with me, I loved the idea of exploring how climate and geopolitical changes are affecting the decision to move abroad and how Americans might approach their move and new life overseas in a fast-changing world.

If you approach this book expecting a guide on relocation or expatriation, what you will discover is far richer: a nuanced exploration of why so many Americans are rethinking where, how, and with whom they live in a world that feels simultaneously more volatile and more interconnected than ever.

I've known Scott for many years, as a friend and more recently as a valued member of the International Asset Management team. In that time, I've witnessed firsthand the discipline, intellect, and curiosity that define his approach. Rather than chase bold proclamations or sensationalism, Scott asks important, practical questions and provides thoughtful answers based on his extensive experience and research. This blend of pragmatism and insight permeates the book.

Today's global landscape is shaped by forces that once seemed distant: climate risk, economic instability, political polarization, technological disruption, and shifting cultural identities. In Adapting Elsewhere, Scott challenges us to overcome our complacency, inviting us not just to assess these forces, but to ask how they impact some of the most fundamental human needs: safety, purpose, belonging, and how to build a life that aligns with our values.

Climate change, in its environmental and metaphorical senses, provided a catalyst for the idea, but this book is not a manifesto of fear or retreat. Instead, it is an honest assessment of how the new realities should shape our decisions about where and how we live in the world.

What makes this book genuinely valuable however, isn't the depiction of challenges; it's the practical information to help Americans moving abroad make informed decisions and adapt.

Adapting Elsewhere demystifies complex but important topics, from financial planning and tax implications to healthcare. These sections are invaluable not just to would-be expats, but to their planners, partners, and families.

Whether you're contemplating the international digital nomad lifestyle, retirement abroad, or a full emigration, this book is more than a practical guide. The chapters on raising children abroad and on cultural identity and belonging are especially insightful, addressing the emotional layers of adapting to a new life abroad - grief, integration, and ultimately, growth.

This holistic approach reflects a truth many of us who work in the cross-border financial planning world understand: moving across borders reshapes who we are and how we think about home, community, and the world. Moving abroad is inevitably challenging, but it also brings profound satisfaction and unforeseen opportunities.

At International Asset Management, we specialise in advising Americans with global lives and cross-border finances, and we understand that every expat's story is unique. In this way, Scott's book aligns beautifully with our philosophy. His deep experience of finances and living abroad brings both precision and compassion to the book. We are honoured that he has joined our team.

As you read, you might find some chapters deeply resonate with your own feelings and aspirations: the allure of a different climate or culture, the desire for a more sustainable way of life, or a way to create a future that feels resilient in the face of uncertainty. As you plan, Scott provides not just information, but a framework for thinking through your choices and aligning your decisions with your values, priorities, and goals.

Ultimately, Adapting Elsewhere reframes a fundamental question that many of us are now asking, "Where should I live?", into something deeper and more empowering: "Where can I thrive in a changing world?"

It's a privilege to introduce this work. It's a resource I believe you will return to again and again, not just for guidance, but for the thoughtful perspective it brings to one of the most significant life decisions we can make, relocating abroad.

Tom Zachystal
President, IAM
(International Asset Management - https://iamadvisors.com/)

PREFACE

This book did not begin as a manifesto or a plan to leave the United States. It began as a series of questions—quiet ones at first, then increasingly insistent. Questions about cost and quality of life, about safety and health, about time and meaning. Questions that many Americans are now asking, often privately, sometimes hesitantly, and rarely all at once.

For much of my life, the idea of living abroad belonged to a different category of imagination. It was something one did after retirement, after obligations were fulfilled, or briefly, as a kind of interlude before returning to "real life." Home was assumed to be fixed. Stability was assumed to be domestic. The future, whatever its challenges, was expected to unfold within familiar borders.

Yet my own life unfolded very differently.

I spent years as an international airline pilot, including being based in Berlin, flying routinely throughout Europe, Asia, South and Central America, and the Middle East. Living across time zones and cultures reshaped how I understood daily life. I saw how different societies organized work, healthcare, family life, aging, and public space, and how many assumptions Americans treat as universal are, in fact, cultural choices.

At the same time, my life beyond aviation deepened that perspective even further. I have sailed extensively around the world, racing offshore and crossing both the Pacific and Atlantic Oceans, and spending years sailing throughout the Mediterranean. Long passages teach a particular kind of clarity. When you are days or weeks from land, comfort is secondary to preparation, adaptability, and judgment. You learn to read systems—weather, water, human behavior—and to respect forces that cannot be negotiated with. That experience mirrors expatriation more closely than most people realize: success depends less on boldness than on planning, humility, and an honest understanding of risk.

In parallel, for more than thirty years, I have worked as an international financial advisor, helping expatriates, globally-mobile professionals, retirees, and cross-border families navigate the practical realities of living abroad. I've seen what looks ideal on paper collapse under real-world friction, and I've seen modest, well-planned moves succeed quietly and sustainably. Over time, a pattern became clear: thriving abroad is rarely about wealth or bravado. It is about alignment—across lifestyle, legal structure, finances, and expectations.

Still, even with this exposure, many of the assumptions Americans carry remained remarkably durable—until they didn't.

Over the past decade, and especially in the years following the pandemic, those assumptions began to feel less secure. Costs rose faster than incomes. Healthcare grew more complex and more adversarial. Climate risks became personal rather than abstract. Political and social polarization seeped into daily life. At the same time, technology quietly dissolved many of the barriers that once made mobility impractical. Work became portable. Information became abundant. Legal pathways, while imperfect, became visible.

What emerged was not a single dramatic moment, but a gradual realization: staying put was no longer the default choice it once seemed to be. Nor, however, was leaving a simple or universally desirable solution. The real question was not whether to stay or go, but how to think clearly about choice itself in a world where conditions are changing faster than institutions.

This book is the result of that inquiry.

It is written for Americans who feel a growing tension between the lives they are living and the lives they imagine might be possible elsewhere. For those who are curious about living abroad but skeptical of glossy narratives and social-media fantasies. For people who want to understand not just where they could go, but what it would actually mean—legally, financially, socially, and emotionally—to build a life across borders.

It is also written with restraint. Living abroad is not a cure-all. It does not eliminate risk, guarantee happiness, or absolve one of responsibility. It introduces new complexities even as it relieves others. This book does not argue that everyone should leave the United States, nor does it present expatriation as a moral or political stance. Instead, it treats mobility as a form of adaptation, one possible response among many to a world in flux.

Throughout these pages, you will encounter themes rather than prescriptions: agency over default, intentionality over inertia, design over reaction. You will read about digital nomads, retirees, families, and long-term emigrants—not as archetypes to emulate, but as examples of how people are negotiating change in real time. You will see how healthcare, education, work, and lifestyle choices intersect in ways that are often invisible until one steps outside familiar systems.

Most importantly, this book invites you to reconsider what "home" means. Not a single place or permanent decision, but an evolving relationship between values, environment, and stage of life. For some, home will remain where it has always been. For others, it will expand to include new places. And for many, it will become something plural—anchored in more than one country, more than one rhythm, more than one way of being.

You do not need to have answers as you begin reading. You do not need to be ready to move, or even want to. This book is not a checklist or a call to action. It is a framework for thinking clearly in uncertain times.

If it succeeds, it will not push you toward a particular destination. It will help you ask better questions about how and where you want to live. And it will remind you of something easy to forget: that choice itself is a form of freedom, and that understanding your options is the first step toward using it wisely.

INTRODUCTION

Stay or Leave–or Both?

Not long ago, the idea of leaving the United States to live abroad occupied a narrow corner of the American imagination. It was something retirees did after a lifetime of work, something artists and romantics dreamed about, or something adventurers attempted briefly before returning home. For most people, it was not a serious option. Life was assumed to unfold within national borders, and stability was understood as something rooted in place.

That assumption no longer holds.

Across generations and professions, Americans are quietly rethinking where life happens. Young professionals untethered from offices, mid-career workers exhausted by cost and pace, retirees recalculating what their savings can realistically support, and families searching for safety and balance are all asking a version of the same question: What does it mean to live well now? Increasingly, the answer they arrive at is not about working harder or optimizing within the system they know. It is about changing the system itself—by changing location.

What was once an escape plan has become, for many, a life strategy.

This book begins with a deceptively simple question (Stay or leave?) and then deliberately complicates it. Because in the modern world, shaped by technology, mobility, and overlapping crises, the more honest question is often, Do I really have to choose? Can a person remain rooted in one country while building a meaningful life in another? Can home be plural rather than singular? Can belonging stretch across borders without breaking?

For a growing number of Americans, the answer is yes.

Living Between: A Personal Geography

For years, my own life has quietly embodied this question. While raising my family in the United States, I have also lived a parallel life in Europe—moving in and out of the Schengen Zone, navigating its ninety-day limits, seasonal rhythms, and legal constraints. What is often referred to casually as the "Schengen shuffle" has, for me, been less a loophole than a long-term experiment, a way of testing places not as destinations, but as environments for living.

Over time, this rhythm—part American, part European—allowed me to build something more valuable than a list of favorite cities. It created a personal database of lived experience: how different places feel in winter versus summer; how bureaucracy functions when you need healthcare or residency paperwork; how communities absorb outsiders over time rather than in weeks; how daily life actually unfolds once novelty fades.

That process gradually narrowed my focus. Rather than chasing variety, I began paying closer attention to depth—particularly in the central Mediterranean, where climate, culture, history, and access converge in distinctive ways. And among those places, Malta emerged not as a fantasy or an accident, but as a deliberate point of gravity: small enough to be navigable, old enough to be layered, stable enough to plan around, and strategically positioned between Europe, North Africa, and the broader Mediterranean world.

This book grows directly out of that lived tension—between staying and leaving, between familiarity and possibility, between one home and several.

The Rise of the Mobile American

The conditions that once made emigration rare have quietly dissolved. Work is no longer inseparable from location. Banking, communication, and even healthcare can be managed across borders. Flights are cheaper, information is abundant, and communities form online long before they do on the ground. What once required severing ties now requires managing them.

As a result, Americans are experimenting. Some live part of the year abroad and return seasonally. Others rotate between countries, adapting to visa rules and climate patterns. Still others establish permanent lives overseas while maintaining legal, financial, and emotional connections to the United States. These are not outliers. They are early participants in a broader shift toward transnational living.

This experimentation is often framed as lifestyle design, but beneath the logistics lies something more serious. The movement is not driven primarily by novelty or wanderlust. It is driven by pressure. By housing costs that outpace incomes. By healthcare systems that feel adversarial rather than protective. By political polarization that seeps into daily life. By environmental risks that are no longer theoretical but personal.

Mobility has become a form of optionality—an insurance policy against instability.

Climate as Catalyst

Climate change is the most visible accelerant of this shift. It is no longer an abstract future threat but a present condition that shapes where people can live safely and affordably. Wildfires, heat waves, water scarcity, floods, and rising insurance costs are already redrawing internal migration patterns within the United States. For some Americans, the realization is unsettling: the places they assumed would always be home may not remain viable.

In response, people begin to think spatially. They ask where water is secure, where temperatures are tolerable, where infrastructure holds. For some, those places still exist within U.S. borders. For others, they do not. Climate resilience becomes a personal calculation rather than a policy abstraction, and borders begin to matter less than conditions.

Yet this book does not argue that there is a perfect refuge. There is none. Every place carries risk. Every system has limits. The question is not where risk disappears, but where it becomes manageable—where quality of life, safety, affordability, and meaning align well enough to sustain a life.

A World in Flux

Climate is only one force reshaping the landscape. Political instability, democratic erosion, widening inequality, and the fraying of civic trust have altered how many Americans feel about the future. The pandemic made visible how quickly systems can fail and how unevenly their failures are distributed. It also demonstrated the value of flexibility—of having options when borders close, economies stall, or institutions falter.

At the same time, the world beyond U.S. borders has become more legible. English is widely spoken. International healthcare systems are accessible. Legal pathways exist for residence, work, and retirement. Living abroad no longer requires abandoning one's identity or cutting ties. It requires learning how to manage complexity.

This is where the old narrative of expatriation breaks down. Leaving no longer means leaving behind. It often means living between.

Redefining Home

At its core, this book is about how Americans are redefining the idea of home. Not as a single place or permanent decision, but as a dynamic relationship between values, environment, and stage of life. For some, home will remain firmly rooted in the United States. For others, it will shift abroad entirely. And for many, it will exist in more than one place, changing over time.

This is not a book about escape. It is a book about adaptation. About recognizing that the world has changed, and that clinging to inherited assumptions about where life must be lived may no longer serve everyone equally well. It is about reclaiming agency in the face of structural change.

In the chapters that follow, we explore how Americans are doing this in practice. We examine work and mobility, retirement and reinvention, emigration and legality, healthcare and education, family life and lifestyle design. We look at the systems that shape daily life abroad—not to romanticize them, but to understand them clearly. We address both the opportunities and the constraints, because living abroad is neither fantasy nor panacea. It is a strategy—one that requires planning, humility, and intention.

As you read, you may recognize yourself in these pages. You may begin to imagine mornings that feel calmer, cities that feel more human-scaled, or a relationship to time that feels less adversarial. You may also feel resistance, uncertainty, or grief at the idea of change. All of these responses are part of the process.

You may discover that the most important realization is not whether you should stay or leave, but that you have more choice than you were taught to believe.

You can stay. You can leave. Or, increasingly, you can do both.

Chapter 1

CLIMATE CHANGE

Part I: The End of Assumptions

For much of the modern era, the decision to move abroad carried an air of romance or ambition. People left home to seek adventure, opportunity, reinvention, or sometimes refuge from political or economic constraint. Climate, by contrast, was assumed. It was background. Stable. Familiar. Something you complained about, adapted to, or escaped for a week or two on vacation—but rarely something that shaped life's largest decisions.

That assumption is quietly dissolving.

Climate change is no longer a distant abstraction reserved for scientific panels, policy debates, or future generations. It has become an active force in daily life, altering not just ecosystems but routines, finances, health, and long-term planning. It intrudes on conversations once considered unrelated: housing affordability, insurance, healthcare access, energy reliability, food prices, even education and retirement. And increasingly, it intrudes on a question that feels both deeply personal and profoundly practical: Where can I still live well?

For many Americans, the unsettling realization is that the answer may no longer be obvious—and may no longer be domestic.

This is not about alarmism. It is about recalibration. It is about recognizing that the environmental conditions that quietly underpinned American prosperity and mobility in the twentieth century are shifting, unevenly but unmistakably. And as those conditions change, so too does the logic of staying put.

This perspective did not emerge for me abstractly. In 2021, I published Investing in a New Climate, a book focused on adaptation, exploring how individuals, institutions, and portfolios navigate a world shaped by accelerating climate, political, and economic change. While researching that work, I spent time in some of the planet's most climate-sensitive regions, including Antarctica and Greenland. There, the reality of warming was no longer theoretical. It was visible, measurable, and immediate.

Standing alongside scientists studying glacial systems, I saw empirical evidence of change that defied historical norms: ice loss occurring on timescales measured not in centuries but in years, melt patterns described by researchers as unprecedented within the span of modern observation. These were not speculative models or distant forecasts; they were lived conditions, unfolding in real time. The experience clarified something essential: climate change is not an event waiting to happen. It is a process already underway, reshaping physical reality faster than most social and economic systems are designed to absorb.

What follows here builds on that realization—not as a scientific treatise, but as a practical inquiry into how environmental stress translates into everyday friction long before it reaches the level of catastrophe. I offer not a call to flee, but an invitation to reassess. To understand how climate stress manifests not as a single dramatic disaster, but as a slow accumulation of pressure—physical, economic, and psychological—that reshapes daily life quietly, persistently, and often invisibly.

Heat as a Structural Force

The most immediate and widely felt expression of climate change in the United States is heat. Not the familiar discomfort of a hot summer afternoon, but prolonged, intense heat that stretches across weeks and months, pressing against the boundaries of what human bodies, infrastructure, and social systems can tolerate.

In cities such as Phoenix, Las Vegas, Dallas, Houston, and increasingly Austin, summer temperatures now regularly exceed levels once considered extreme. Heat indexes above 100 degrees Fahrenheit are no longer anomalies. They are becoming the baseline. Nights offer little relief, remaining warm enough to disrupt sleep and prevent buildings from cooling. Outdoor labor becomes dangerous, sometimes lethal. Emergency rooms see spikes in heat-related illness that disproportionately affect the elderly, the chronically ill, and those without reliable access to cooling.

What makes heat uniquely destabilizing is not merely its intensity, but its persistence. A single heatwave can be endured; a season defined by heat becomes something else entirely—a chronic condition rather than an acute event. Daily life adjusts around it. Walking becomes strategic. Social activity is compressed into early mornings and late evenings. Children are kept indoors. Power bills climb. Air conditioning shifts from convenience to necessity.

Yet even that necessity exposes vulnerability. Electrical grids strained by peak demand falter with increasing frequency. Rolling blackouts, once rare in many regions, are now part of summer planning. For households already stretched by rising housing and healthcare costs, the financial burden of staying cool becomes significant. The price of survival quietly rises.

Heat also compounds other environmental stresses. It worsens air quality by accelerating the formation of ground-level ozone and intensifying wildfire smoke. It degrades roads, buckles rail lines, and shortens the lifespan of infrastructure designed for cooler climates. Schools close. Work hours shift. Productivity declines. The economic effects ripple outward, often invisibly.

Over time, heat changes not just how people live, but where it makes sense to live at all.

The Geography of Unease

Historically, Americans have been remarkably mobile. The postwar decades saw waves of internal migration driven by industry, housing, and lifestyle preference. Sunbelt states boomed precisely because climate was seen as an asset—warm winters, abundant land, and the promise of year-round livability.

That calculation is now under strain.

In many parts of the southern and southwestern United States, the number of days each year that exceed safe heat thresholds is rising sharply. What was once manageable with adaptation—better insulation, improved cooling, altered schedules—is edging toward something more existential. At certain extremes, the human body simply cannot cool itself effectively, even in shade, even with hydration. These limits are physiological, not political.

The consequences are unevenly distributed. Wealthier households can buffer themselves with newer construction, solar panels, backup batteries, and higher utility bills. Others cannot. Neighborhoods diverge. Inequality deepens. Climate stress becomes a sorting mechanism, reinforcing existing disparities.

This matters because climate change does not require universal catastrophe to drive migration. It only requires sufficient friction—enough discomfort, enough cost, enough uncertainty—that people begin to imagine alternatives.

Once that imagining begins, it tends to spread.

Water, or the Lack of It

Heat rarely travels alone. It is accompanied, paradoxically, by water, either too little or too much.

In the American West, drought has become a defining feature of the landscape. Reservoirs fluctuate at historic lows. Snowpack, once a reliable natural storage system, melts earlier and more erratically. Rivers that support agriculture, cities, and ecosystems are increasingly overallocated, their future dependent on legal agreements forged in a very different climate era.

For households, water stress shows up in mundane but unsettling ways: restrictions on lawn watering, rising utility rates, debates over new development, and quiet anxiety about long-term availability. Water stress threatens the livelihoods of farmers and constrains the growth of cities. For entire regions, it raises uncomfortable questions about sustainability.

At the same time, other parts of the country are experiencing the opposite problem. Heavier rainfall events overwhelm drainage systems designed for gentler patterns. Flooding becomes more frequent, more damaging, and less predictable. Infrastructure built to manage twentieth-century weather struggles to cope with twenty-first-century extremes.

The result is a sense of instability that transcends any single event. People notice when roads flood repeatedly, when basements become uninhabitable, when insurance premiums spike or coverage disappears altogether. These are not dramatic disasters; they are slow erosions of confidence in place. Once lost, this confidence is difficult to restore.

When Climate Becomes Personal

What distinguishes the current moment from earlier environmental challenges is not merely scale, but intimacy. Climate change now touches aspects of life that feel deeply personal: health, home, family routines, and financial planning.

Parents worry about children playing outside in extreme heat or breathing smoke-filled air. Older adults find themselves more vulnerable to temperature swings and power outages. Homeowners confront the uneasy realization that their most significant investment may be exposed to risks they did not price in—or cannot insure against.

Even those insulated by wealth and flexibility sense the shift. Travel plans are disrupted by fires, floods, and storms. Second homes become liabilities. Retirement destinations begin to feel less secure. The idea of "aging in place" becomes more complicated when the place itself is changing.

This is how climate change moves from theory to motivation. Not through abstract charts or distant projections, but through lived experience that accumulates year by year.

People begin to ask questions they never had to ask before. How reliable is the grid here? How secure is the water supply? What happens if insurance disappears? What happens if summers keep getting hotter? What happens if this place becomes harder, not easier, to live in as I age?

Once asked, these questions rarely stay contained.

Part II: When Adaptation Isn't Enough

If heat represents the most visceral signal of climate change, water may be the most destabilizing. It moves slowly, insinuating itself into systems that once felt permanent—coastlines, aquifers, drainage networks, insurance markets—until those systems begin to fail not spectacularly, but persistently.

For Americans living near the coast, the transformation is already underway. Sea-level rise is no longer a future projection traced in scientific journals. It is visible in flooded streets on clear days, corroded infrastructure, and saltwater creeping into places it does not belong. In parts of Florida, what locals once called "nuisance flooding" has become a regular disruption, altering traffic patterns, damaging property, and eroding the assumption that coastal living is a lifestyle choice rather than a calculated risk.

The physical changes are troubling enough. The secondary effects are more consequential.

As seawater pushes inland, freshwater aquifers—the invisible reservoirs that sustain cities—become contaminated. Roads deteriorate from repeated exposure to brackish water. Septic systems fail. Electrical substations corrode. Each fix becomes more expensive than the last, and none offer permanence. The water keeps coming.

Insurance companies, designed to price risk dispassionately, are often the first institutions to respond. In high-risk coastal zones, insurers have begun to withdraw coverage altogether or raise premiums to levels that render properties effectively uninsurable. When insurance disappears, mortgages become difficult or impossible to obtain. Property values stagnate or decline. Local tax bases weaken, reducing the funds available for adaptation and repair. A feedback loop emerges—quiet at first, then unmistakable.

Homeowners discover that climate risk is not merely environmental: it is financial. It lives on balance sheets and loan agreements, in premiums and exclusions, in the fine print that governs whether rebuilding is possible after the next storm. What once felt like a manageable inconvenience becomes a source of chronic uncertainty.

And uncertainty, more than catastrophe, is what drives people to reconsider where they live.

Infrastructure Under Stress

Much of the United States' physical infrastructure—roads, bridges, power grids, water systems—was built during an era of relative climatic predictability. Design standards assumed ranges of temperature, rainfall, and storm intensity that no longer hold.

Heat degrades asphalt and warps rails. Flooding overwhelms drainage systems. Power lines sag under thermal stress. Electrical and water substations flood. Pipelines rupture as soil shifts. Each failure is treated as an isolated problem and repaired or patched, often at great expense. Collectively, they point to a deeper issue: adaptation is lagging behind change.

This has consequences for daily life. Power outages become more common. Water main breaks increase. Transportation disruptions ripple through supply chains. The reliability that underpins modern living—turning on a tap, flipping a switch, trusting that systems will function—erodes incrementally.

People notice. They adjust. And eventually, some begin to ask whether adaptation alone is enough.

The Myth of the Safe Zone

For years, discussions of climate migration focused on the idea of "safe havens." Regions thought to be insulated from extreme heat, sea-level rise, or hurricanes—often the American Midwest or parts of the interior Northeast—were imagined as future destinations for those fleeing more vulnerable areas. That narrative is being revised.

The climate system is not simply warming; it is destabilizing. Patterns that once held—predictable rainfall, seasonal temperature swings, storm paths—are breaking down. The result is not a clear map of winners and losers, but a mosaic of shifting risks.

The Midwest, long regarded as climatically stable, has experienced increasingly severe flooding events as warmer air holds more moisture and releases it in intense bursts. Rivers overflow more frequently. Agricultural fields flood at critical points in the growing season. Infrastructure designed for steadier precipitation struggles to cope. Meanwhile, hotter summers place new stress on populations and industries unaccustomed to prolonged heat.

In the West, wildfire risk has expanded dramatically, reaching into mountain towns and suburban fringes once considered safe. Smoke travels thousands of miles, degrading air quality far from the flames themselves. A fire season that once lasted weeks now stretches across months, turning summer skies an unsettling orange and forcing people indoors.

Even colder regions are not immune. The destabilization of the jet stream has produced more frequent and intense cold snaps, such as the polar vortex events that have crippled Texas and strained heating systems across much of the country. These episodes reveal vulnerabilities in infrastructure built for historical norms rather than emerging extremes.

What is now clear is that climate change does not respect regional reputations. It exposes weaknesses where systems were optimized for stability rather than resilience.

The Psychological Shift

Migration is often portrayed as a dramatic response to sudden disaster. In reality, it is more often the product of slow psychological accumulation. A sense that life is becoming harder, more expensive, more constrained—not because of personal failure, but because of environmental conditions beyond individual control.

At first, people adapt. They install better insulation. They upgrade air conditioning. They invest in generators or backup batteries. They alter routines, avoid certain seasons, accept new inconveniences as the cost of staying put.

But adaptation has limits. It requires capital, attention, and emotional bandwidth. It assumes that the underlying system will eventually stabilize. When that assumption weakens, adaptation begins to feel like delay rather than solution.

This is the moment when the idea of exit enters the conversation—not out of panic, but from prudence.

For many Americans, this shift is subtle. It surfaces in casual remarks about summers becoming unbearable, about insurance premiums rising too fast, about infrastructure that feels increasingly fragile. It appears in retirement planning conversations, in second-home decisions, in questions about where children might want to settle.

Importantly, this reconsideration is not confined to those at the margins. It is occurring among the middle and upper-middle classes—people with resources, education, and mobility. They are not being forced out. They are choosing to look ahead. That choice reframes migration itself.

From Adaptation to Optionality

What distinguishes climate-driven relocation in wealthy countries from displacement elsewhere is optionality. Those with means can plan. They can compare. They can move before necessity hardens into urgency.

This does not make the decision trivial. Leaving familiar places, social networks, and cultural anchors carries its own cost. But for a growing number of people, the cost of staying—financially, physically, emotionally—feels increasingly uncertain.

The idea of remaining indefinitely in a region facing escalating climate stress begins to feel less like stability and more like inertia.

At this point, the question shifts. It is no longer simply how to adapt to change, but where adaptation is most likely to succeed. Which societies are investing proactively in resilience? Which governments are planning for long-term climate realities rather than reacting piecemeal? Which places offer not immunity, but manageability?

This is where climate change intersects with geopolitics, governance, and global inequality—and where the concept of expatriation evolves from lifestyle choice to strategic positioning.

Part III: Choosing the Ground Beneath Your Feet

By the time climate change becomes a factor in relocation decisions, something fundamental has already shifted. The question is no longer whether the climate is changing, but whether the places we inhabit are equipped to manage that change in ways that preserve quality of life.

This distinction matters. Climate change does not operate in isolation. Its consequences are filtered through political systems, infrastructure choices, social norms, and economic priorities. Two regions can face similar environmental pressures and experience radically different outcomes depending on how well they anticipate, absorb, and adapt.

It is here, at the intersection of environment and governance, that climate expatriation—the idea of leaving one's home as a result of climate change—begins to make sense.

For a growing number of Americans, the idea of moving abroad is not rooted in dissatisfaction with the United States as a country, but in a sober assessment of how unevenly climate risk is being addressed within it. Planning horizons are short. Infrastructure investment is fragmented. Insurance markets are retreating faster than public policy can respond. Responsibility for adaptation often falls to individuals, even when the challenges are systemic. This creates a quiet but powerful incentive to look elsewhere.

Livability Over Optimism

In earlier eras, migration was often driven by optimism—belief in upward mobility, economic expansion, or cultural reinvention. Climate-driven migration is more pragmatic, shaped by the desire for livability rather than growth, stability rather than acceleration.

Livability is a deceptively simple concept. It encompasses temperature ranges that allow for daily life without constant mitigation, reliable access to water and energy, urban design that reduces exposure to extremes rather than amplifying them, healthcare systems capable of absorbing climate-related stress, and social cohesion that buffers shocks rather than magnifying them.

Some countries have invested in these qualities not because they anticipated climate migration, but because their political cultures emphasize long-term planning and public good. In parts of Europe, for example, dense cities were built before the dominance of automobiles, resulting in walkability and lower per-capita energy use. Strong social safety nets reduce vulnerability during disruptions. Public healthcare systems are structured to handle population-wide stress rather than individual financial risk.

These features, once seen as cultural preferences, now function as climate assets.

Countries such as Portugal, Slovenia, and parts of Northern Europe are increasingly attractive not because they are untouched by climate change—they are not—but because they offer more moderate climates combined with governance structures oriented toward resilience. Heat exists, but within tolerable bounds. Flooding occurs, but within systems designed to manage it. Adaptation is collective rather than privatized.

Nations in the Southern Hemisphere, such as Uruguay or certain regions of Chile, offer a different kind of appeal. Geographic insulation, political stability, and temperate climates intersect with a slower pace of life that reduces exposure to the relentless stressors of climate-affected megacities. These places are not utopias. Their risks feel comprehensible rather than compounding.

The Role of Institutions

What often distinguishes destinations as viable rather than merely attractive is institutional competence. Climate resilience is less about eliminating risk than about managing it transparently and equitably.

When people consider expatriation in this context, they are implicitly evaluating trust. Trust that power grids will function during heatwaves. Trust that water systems are monitored and protected. Trust that healthcare will be available without financial ruin. Trust that governments are capable of acting decisively when conditions change.

In the United States, trust varies dramatically by region. In some areas, robust investment and planning have produced meaningful adaptation. In others, political polarization and fiscal constraints have slowed response, leaving residents to navigate risk largely on their own.

Looking abroad introduces new trade-offs, but it also introduces alternatives—places where climate risk is integrated into long-term planning rather than deferred to future crises.

Looking abroad does not mean abandoning one's country. It means expanding the range of choices available to oneself and one's family.

Climate Migration Without the Drama

One of the most persistent misconceptions about climate migration is that it will arrive suddenly, in waves, driven by disaster. In reality, among affluent populations, it is already quietly unfolding.

People begin by spending more time elsewhere. They test different climates during different seasons. They explore residency options. They diversify assets internationally. They establish optionality—not as an escape plan, but as a hedge.

This gradualism is significant. It reflects the fact that climate expatriation is not primarily about fear. It is about foresight.

Those who move first are often the least visible: retirees seeking temperate weather and reliable healthcare; remote workers able to decouple income from location; families prioritizing long-term stability over short-term familiarity. Their decisions rarely make headlines, but they shape demographic patterns, nonetheless.

Over time, these individual choices aggregate into broader shifts. Demand rises in certain regions. Infrastructure adapts. Cultural bridges form. Migration networks deepen. What begins as personal strategy becomes structural change.

Redefining Home

Perhaps the most profound implication of climate-driven expatriation is how it reshapes the concept of home. For generations, home was assumed to be fixed—a place inherited, purchased, or built, anchored by geography and memory. Climate change has introduced fluidity, refiguring home as something more dynamic: a place chosen not only for emotional resonance, but for its capacity to support life over time. This does not diminish attachment; it reframes it. One can love a place and still acknowledge that it may not be the best place to remain indefinitely.

This reframing is uncomfortable, particularly in cultures that equate permanence with commitment. Yet it mirrors a broader reality of the twenty-first century, in which careers, identities, and communities are increasingly portable.

Climate change accelerates this shift by imposing constraints that cannot be wished away. It asks not where we have always lived, but where living will remain viable.

Acting Without Panic

To consider climate expatriation is not to surrender to inevitability, but to engage with reality deliberately rather than reactively. Where and how we choose to live is no longer merely a matter of preference: it is a strategic decision that deserves the same care, foresight, and honesty we apply to any other long-term commitment.

There is no universal answer, no perfect refuge. Every location carries risk. The difference lies in how those risks are distributed, managed, and mitigated.

For some, the right response will be deepened investment in local resilience—retrofitting homes, advocating for infrastructure upgrades, building community networks. For others, it will involve partial relocation, seasonal living, or eventual departure. The point is not uniformity, but agency.

The decision to move or to remain need not be framed as loss. It can be framed as alignment: between values and environment, between expectations and reality, between the life one hopes to live and the systems that make that life possible. In a warming world, home is not just where we are, but where we can thrive.

Chapter 2

THE GLOBAL ECONOMY

CHOOSING STABILITY IN AN UNSTABLE WORLD

Part I: After the Center Holds

My paternal grandfather left Eastern Europe at the end of the nineteenth century, not out of romantic ambition but economic necessity. He was a cabinet maker by trade, living in a small town near the border of what is now Romania and Moldova. The regional economy was collapsing. Opportunity was narrowing. Political uncertainty and economic stagnation made the future increasingly untenable.

He left with little certainty and no guarantees, traveling first through England, then Canada, and finally arriving in San Francisco. The transition was not easy. He arrived with limited resources and few connections. Yet over time, he established a small business, earned a living, and eventually accumulated enough stability to bring nearly his entire family to the United States.

He did not leave one place because it was uninhabitable; he left because its economic system no longer worked. He chose to participate in a thriving economy rather than remain bound to a failing one.

That decision—made more than a century ago—captures a recurring truth: climate shapes the physical conditions of life, but the economy shapes almost everything else: where jobs exist; where capital flows; which currencies can be trusted; which governments can respond to crisis, and which merely manage decline. If climate determines whether a place remains livable, the economy determines whether life there remains workable.

For much of the period following World War II, Americans rarely needed to think about this distinction. The United States sat at the center of the global economic system, not merely participating in it but defining it. The dollar anchored global trade. American consumers drove demand. American financial markets set the tempo for growth, risk, and innovation worldwide. To live in the United States was, almost by default, to live inside the most stable economic ecosystem on earth.

That assumption—like the assumption of climatic stability—is no longer guaranteed.

This does not mean the American economy is collapsing. It is not. By nearly every traditional metric—gross domestic product, technological innovation, capital market depth, military power—the United States remains a global heavyweight. But the nature of dominance has changed. What once felt permanent now feels conditional. What once felt insulated now feels exposed.

For Americans contemplating expatriation, this shift matters deeply. Economic systems are not abstractions. They determine how easily one can find work, access healthcare, secure housing, protect savings, and plan for the future. They influence immigration policy, social cohesion, and the capacity of governments to absorb shocks—from pandemics to wars to climate disasters.

In an era of accelerating global change, the question is no longer simply, "Where can I live?" It is, "Where does the system still work?"

The Long Arc of American Economic Centrality

To understand why this question feels newly urgent, it helps to recall just how extraordinary the American position has been.

In the aftermath of World War II, much of the industrialized world lay in ruins. The United States emerged not only intact but ascendant, holding the majority of the world's gold reserves, producing an outsized share of global manufacturing, and wielding unparalleled political and financial influence. The Bretton Woods system formalized this reality, placing the dollar at the heart of global trade and finance.

For decades, this arrangement created a virtuous cycle. Global demand for dollars supported American borrowing. American borrowing fueled consumption. Consumption drove global growth. Crises occurred, but the system bent rather than broke, and the United States remained the default refuge when uncertainty spiked.

Even as manufacturing moved offshore and globalization accelerated, the underlying structure held. The United States specialized in finance, services, technology, and intellectual property. Its capital markets absorbed shocks that would have crippled smaller economies. Its currency remained the world's reserve not because it was flawless, but because there was no viable alternative.

This long era of economic centrality shaped American expectations. It encouraged risk-taking. It allowed deficits to grow with relatively little consequence. It fostered the belief—often unspoken—that whatever turbulence arose elsewhere, the United States would remain the safest place to stand.

The past two decades have begun to challenge that belief.

Cracks, Not Collapse

The global financial crisis of 2008 marked the first major rupture in the postwar economic narrative. It exposed deep vulnerabilities within the American financial system and shattered the illusion that sophisticated markets were inherently self-correcting. Although the United States recovered faster than many countries, the social and political aftershocks were profound.

Trust eroded. Inequality widened. Faith in institutions weakened. And critically, the crisis revealed how interconnected—and fragile—the global economy had become.

Since then, shocks have arrived with increasing frequency. A global pandemic exposed the brittleness of just-in-time supply chains. Trade wars disrupted long-standing relationships. Energy shocks rippled through Europe following geopolitical conflict. Climate-related disasters imposed mounting costs on public budgets and private insurers alike.

None of these events, taken alone, signaled the end of American economic leadership. Together, they suggest a system under strain.

National debt has grown beyond levels once considered unthinkable—not because of a single policy failure, but because political consensus around long-term fiscal discipline has eroded. Budget negotiations lurch from crisis to crisis. Structural reforms are deferred. The burden is quietly shifted forward.

Housing affordability has deteriorated across major metropolitan areas, transforming homeownership from a cornerstone of middle-class stability into a source of anxiety. Healthcare costs continue to outpace inflation, imposing hidden taxes on workers and retirees alike. Labor markets strain under demographic shifts and technological disruption, even as productivity gains accrue unevenly.

The result is not collapse, but exposure of cracks in our systems—a narrowing margin for error. Shocks once absorbed with confidence now linger longer, cut deeper, and provoke sharper political conflict.

From Globalization to Fragmentation

At the same time, the global environment in which the U.S. economy operates has fundamentally changed.

The era of seamless globalization—characterized by ever-expanding trade, frictionless capital movement, and tightly integrated supply chains—is giving way to something more fragmented. Nations reassess dependencies. Corporations prioritize resilience over efficiency. Governments speak openly of "de-risking" rather than optimizing.

This shift is pragmatic rather than ideological. Recent crises revealed that concentration carries risk. Supply chains stretched across continents proved brittle under stress. Strategic industries—from semiconductors to energy—are being pulled closer to home or diversified across friendly jurisdictions.

For the United States, this reordering presents both opportunity and constraint. It reinforces the importance of domestic production and technological leadership, while reducing the automatic advantages once conferred by scale and centrality. Competition intensifies. Alliances matter more. Economic power becomes increasingly contingent.

In this environment, economic stability is no longer evenly distributed and must be actively maintained.

Why This Matters for Individuals

For many Americans, global economic shifts can feel remote—something that happens in markets or ministries rather than living rooms. Yet their effects are pervasive.

They shape interest rates and inflation, influencing the affordability of housing and the real value of savings. They affect immigration policy, determining who can move where and under what conditions. They influence public investment in infrastructure, healthcare, and education. They even shape social mood—confidence or anxiety, cohesion or polarization.

When an economic system functions well, it fades into the background. When it falters, it becomes impossible to ignore.

For those considering life abroad, the economy is not merely a backdrop to lifestyle. It is the scaffolding that supports—or undermines—everything else. A temperate climate loses its appeal if savings are eroded by inflation. A vibrant culture offers little comfort if healthcare is inaccessible. Low costs mean little if currency instability destroys purchasing power.

Choosing where to live in the twenty-first century increasingly means choosing which economic risks you are willing to bear—and which you would rather avoid.

The End of Automatic Assumptions

Just as climate change forces a reckoning with environmental assumptions, economic fragmentation forces a reckoning with financial assumptions: that the United States will always be the safest harbor, that the dollar will always dominate, that domestic instability will always be offset by global confidence.

These assumptions may persist longer than critics expect—or they may erode gradually, imperceptibly, until their absence is finally felt.

For individuals with mobility, the question becomes not whether to abandon one system for another, but how to position oneself intelligently within a changing landscape. How to diversify exposure. How to seek stability without paralysis. How to balance loyalty with foresight.

This is the space in which expatriation becomes an economic strategy rather than a lifestyle choice—a way to align personal circumstances with systems that feel more predictable, more resilient, or simply better suited to long-term goals.

Let us now examine what economic stability looks like in practice, how different regions are navigating global disruption, and how individuals can evaluate not only where opportunity exists today, but where it is most likely to endure.

Part II: Where Systems Still Hold

Once the idea of economic stability moves from abstraction to personal concern, the world looks different. Countries are no longer evaluated solely by their beauty, culture, or even climate, but by the quiet reliability of their systems. How consistently do institutions function? How predictable are the rules? How well does the economy absorb stress without forcing ordinary people to carry the cost?

These questions matter because economic disruption rarely announces itself with collapse. More often, it reveals itself through friction: a bank transfer that suddenly takes longer, a tax rule that changes midstream, a healthcare bill that arrives unexpectedly, a currency that loses purchasing power just fast enough to undermine planning but not fast enough to trigger panic.

For Americans considering expatriation, the goal is not to outrun risk—risk exists everywhere—but to live within systems where risk is managed transparently and distributed fairly.

Europe's Quiet Strength

Despite periodic crises and endless commentary about bureaucracy, Europe continues to offer one of the world's most durable economic environments for residents. This durability does not stem from explosive growth or entrepreneurial mythmaking. It comes from institutional depth.

In much of Western and Northern Europe, economic life is structured around continuity rather than acceleration. Governments plan in decades, not election cycles. Public infrastructure is maintained with an eye toward longevity. Healthcare is treated as a public good rather than a consumer product. Labor protections, while sometimes criticized for rigidity, provide stability during downturns rather than amplifying them.

For expatriates, this stability translates into a sense of predictability that is difficult to quantify but easy to feel. Costs may be higher on paper, particularly in taxes, but they are offset by reduced exposure to catastrophic expenses. One rarely worries about losing healthcare coverage, being bankrupted by illness, or navigating opaque systems alone.

Countries such as Portugal illustrate how this model can coexist with openness. As a member of the European Union and the Eurozone, Portugal benefits from monetary stability and regulatory alignment with some of the world's largest economies. At the same time, it has pursued policies that attract foreign residents, remote workers, and retirees, leveraging international capital without surrendering institutional coherence.

The result is not rapid growth but steady normalization. Inflation remains manageable. Public debt, once a concern, has been brought under control through reforms and European oversight. The economy does not promise riches, but it offers reliability—and in uncertain times, reliability has its own appeal.

Germany represents the other end of the European spectrum: industrial, export-driven, methodical. It is not a country that sells itself on lifestyle fantasy, but on competence. Infrastructure works. Rules are enforced. Institutions function. The social contract is explicit and, for the most part, honored.

For American expats, Germany can feel demanding. Taxes are high. Bureaucracy is real. Integration requires effort. But in return, there is clarity. One knows where one stands. One knows what to expect. In an unstable world, that clarity is not trivial.

The Appeal of Smaller, Well-Run States

Beyond Europe's major economies, a number of smaller countries have emerged as quiet beneficiaries of global instability. These nations lack the scale to dominate, but they compensate with governance quality, fiscal discipline, and social cohesion.

Switzerland is the archetype. Its neutrality, decentralized political structure, and conservative fiscal management have insulated it from many global shocks. Inflation remains low. Institutions are deeply trusted. The Swiss franc is widely regarded as a safe-haven currency.

For expatriates, Switzerland offers exceptional security—personal, financial, and institutional. The cost, however, is significant. Living there requires either substantial income or careful planning. It is not a place for arbitrage. It is a place for preservation.

Canada occupies a different niche. Resource-rich, politically moderate, and institutionally stable, it has navigated global volatility with relative calm. Its banking system is tightly regulated. Public services are broadly accessible. Immigration policy is structured rather than reactive.

Canada's economic exposure to commodities introduces some currency volatility, but its fundamentals remain sound. For Americans, Canada offers a familiar cultural environment with a different social contract—one that prioritizes collective stability over individual optimization.

Australia and New Zealand extend this pattern into the Southern Hemisphere. Both countries combine strong institutions with geographic insulation and access to Asia-Pacific growth. Their economies are advanced, their governance relatively stable, and their societies cohesive.

They are not immune to climate risk, nor are they inexpensive. But they offer something increasingly rare: the sense that the system is paying attention to long-term risk rather than merely managing short-term optics.

Where Volatility Hides Behind Charm

Not all attractive destinations offer economic security. Some offer lifestyle advantages that mask underlying fragility.

Latin America, for example, presents a complex picture. Countries such as Argentina captivate with culture, food, and urban sophistication. Yet its economic history is marked by repeated debt crises, currency collapses, and inflationary spirals. These cycles erode trust, undermine savings, and make long-term planning an exercise in improvisation.

Living well in such environments often requires local knowledge, flexibility, and a willingness to operate partially outside formal systems. For short-term living or cultural immersion, this may be acceptable; for retirement or wealth preservation, it carries real risk.

Turkey offers another cautionary tale. Strategically located, historically rich, and culturally vibrant, it has nonetheless suffered from persistent inflation, policy unpredictability, and political centralization. Currency depreciation has punished savers and distorted pricing. Rules shift. Confidence wavers.

In parts of Africa, Asia, and Southern Europe, similar trade-offs emerge. Beauty and affordability coexist with bureaucratic opacity, weak currencies, or underfunded public services. None of these factors is disqualifying in isolation. Together, they demand careful consideration.

The danger lies not in volatility itself, but in underestimating it.

Rethinking "Opportunity"

One of the most difficult adjustments for Americans contemplating expatriation is redefining opportunity. In the United States, opportunity is often equated with upside: growth, scale, and the possibility of outsized returns. This mindset aligns well with a dynamic, risk-tolerant economy.

Abroad, particularly in more stable societies, opportunity may look different. It may involve lower ceilings but higher floors. Slower growth but greater security. Fewer spectacular wins but fewer catastrophic losses.

For many, this trade-off becomes more appealing with age, family responsibilities, or accumulated assets. The question shifts from "How much can I make?" to "How much do I need to protect?" This shift does not signal retreat. It signals recalibration.

Choosing stability is not a lack of ambition. It is a form of strategy—one that recognizes that wealth, health, and peace of mind are easier to preserve than to rebuild.

The Personal Nature of Economic Risk

Ultimately, no country can be labeled universally "safe" or "unsafe." Economic stability is relational. It depends on income sources, assets, citizenship status, family structure, and personal tolerance for uncertainty.

A young entrepreneur may thrive in a volatile but fast-growing market. A retiree on a fixed income may find the same environment intolerable. A remote worker earning in dollars may benefit from currency arbitrage—until inflation erodes local services or policy shifts restrict access.

Understanding this requires moving beyond headlines and rankings. It requires imagining daily life under stress. How would you pay for healthcare? How would you access cash? How would inflation affect rent, food, or utilities? How quickly could rules change—and how exposed would you be if they did?

These are not theoretical exercises. They are the quiet calculus behind every successful expatriation story—and every failed one.

Now, let's turn from national systems to personal strategy, to explore currency risk, income diversification, and the concept of economic sovereignty—not as abstract finance, but as tools for living well in an unstable world.

Part III: Economic Sovereignty in an Age of Volatility

By the time someone seriously considers relocating abroad for economic reasons, the decision is rarely ideological. It is practical. It grows out of a desire for predictability, for a system that allows long-term planning without constant recalibration. At its core, this desire reflects something deeper than tax efficiency or cost of living: it reflects a search for economic sovereignty.

Economic sovereignty, at the personal level, is not about rejecting one country in favor of another. It is about reducing exposure to forces beyond one's control. It is about building a life in which income, savings, healthcare, and daily expenses are not all hostage to a single political or monetary system. In a world where volatility has become structural rather than episodic, this kind of sovereignty is no longer a luxury. It is a form of resilience.

Living Inside a Currency

One of the most overlooked aspects of expatriation is that when you move abroad, you do not simply change addresses. You move into a different monetary environment. Every transaction—rent, groceries, utilities, healthcare—becomes a function of a currency whose behavior may be very different from the U.S. dollar.

For Americans who have lived their entire lives inside a dominant reserve currency, this adjustment can be subtle but profound. The dollar's strength has long acted as an invisible cushion. Inflation abroad mattered less when income was dollar-denominated. Currency swings were curiosities, not existential concerns.

That cushion cannot be assumed indefinitely.

Currency risk does not announce itself with collapse. It creeps in through erosion. A country with high inflation may still feel affordable at first, especially to someone earning in dollars. Over time, however, local prices adjust. Services deteriorate. Skilled professionals emigrate. The quality of what money buys declines, even if nominal costs remain low.

Conversely, living in a stable currency zone—such as the euro area or Switzerland—can feel more expensive on paper but more reliable in practice. Purchasing power holds. Contracts are predictable. Savings retain value. Planning becomes easier.

This is why the choice of destination cannot be separated from the choice of currency. You are not just choosing where to live. You are choosing the unit in which your life will be priced.

Inflation as a Daily Experience

Inflation is often discussed as a macroeconomic statistic. For residents, it is a lived experience.

In high-inflation environments, daily life becomes tactical. Prices change frequently. Long-term contracts are rare or indexed. Trust in institutions weakens as people learn that tomorrow's value may not resemble today's. Savings are converted into hard assets, foreign currencies, or anything that might retain value.

This kind of environment rewards agility but punishes stability. It favors those who can arbitrage systems over those who rely on them. For expatriates seeking peace of mind rather than constant vigilance, this trade-off matters.

By contrast, low-inflation societies foster different behaviors. People plan. They save. They invest in education and infrastructure because the future feels legible. Even when growth is modest, stability allows life to unfold without constant economic triage.

Choosing such an environment is not about avoiding reality, but choosing which realities you are willing to live with every day.

Income, Assets, and Optionality

Economic sovereignty also depends on where income originates and how assets are structured. Many modern expatriates maintain income streams that are geographically decoupled from residence: remote work, pensions, investment income, business ownership.

This decoupling can be powerful. Earning in a strong currency while spending in a more affordable one can enhance one's quality of life dramatically. But it also introduces dependencies. If income depends on a single employer, platform, or regulatory regime, optionality may be more fragile than it appears.

Successful long-term expatriation often involves diversification—not just of investments, but of exposure. Multiple income streams. Assets held in more than one jurisdiction. Access to more than one healthcare system. Sometimes, even multiple residencies or citizenships.

These layers are not about excess. They are about redundancy. Just as resilient systems are designed with backups, resilient lives are built with alternatives. This does not require wealth in the traditional sense. It requires foresight, planning, and a willingness to think in systems rather than snapshots.

The Emotional Side of Stability

Economic decisions are never purely financial. They carry emotional weight. Security is not only about numbers; it is about how safe one feels navigating daily life.

In unstable economies, even small disruptions can feel exhausting. A delayed payment. A policy change. A rumor of capital controls. Each requires attention, adaptation, and stress. Over time, this wears down even the most adventurous spirits.

In stable environments, the absence of drama becomes a feature. One notices not what is exciting, but what is missing: constant vigilance, financial anxiety, the sense of being one policy shift away from upheaval.

For many expatriates, this emotional relief is as valuable as any financial gain. It frees cognitive space for relationships, creativity, health, and purpose.

Choosing Where to Land

By this point, the question of expatriation is no longer about escaping decline or chasing advantage. It is about alignment.

Alignment between climate and comfort. Between economic systems and personal finances. Between governance and values. Between the pace of the world and the pace at which one wants to live.

There is no universal answer. For some, the United States will remain the best place to navigate uncertainty, particularly for those embedded in its innovation economy or supported by strong local institutions. For others, stability may be found abroad—in countries that prioritize continuity over spectacle, resilience over growth, and collective planning over individual improvisation.

What matters is intentionality.

The mistake is not staying. The mistake is assuming that systems will function as they always have, that stability will reassert itself without effort, that waiting carries no cost.

The global economy is not ending. It is reorganizing: power is diffusing, risk is being redistributed. Opportunities still exist, but they are more conditional, more context-dependent, more uneven.

In such a world, choosing where to live is no longer merely a lifestyle decision. It is a form of strategy.

Looking Ahead

In the chapters that follow, we will move from theory to practice. We will explore how to evaluate countries not just for today, but for the decades ahead. How to structure finances across borders. How to think about healthcare, residency, taxation, and legal status. How to build a life abroad that is not only enjoyable, but durable.

Climate change alters the physical terrain of our lives. The global economy shapes the systems that make life possible. Together, they define the contours of choice in the twenty-first century.

The world is changing. You get to choose where you stand within it.

Chapter 3

THE POLITICS OF PLACE

Part I: When Politics Stops Being Background Noise

My friend Su left mainland China at the age of ten.

She was not part of an organized migration program, nor was her departure legal in any meaningful sense. One night, under cover of darkness, her parents placed her beneath a tarp on a small fishing boat bound for Hong Kong. She was alone. The journey was dangerous. Discovery would have meant imprisonment or worse—not only for her, but also for the family she left behind.

Her parents made a choice that many never have to contemplate: to send their child away alone in order to give her a chance at political safety. They were poor. They had little leverage. But they understood something fundamental: under an oppressive political system, neither economic effort nor personal discipline could reliably secure a future.

Su eventually made her way to the United States. She built a life that would have been unimaginable had she remained where she was born. She became a flight attendant for a U.S. airline, gained mobility and independence, and later built a successful career as a real estate entrepreneur. Her story is not merely one of personal resilience. It is an illustration of what happens when political conditions determine whether effort is rewarded or rendered irrelevant.

She did not leave because of climate. She did not leave because of economics alone. She left to escape politics. That distinction matters.

Climate determines whether a place is habitable. The economy determines whether life there is workable. Politics determines whether either of those conditions can be trusted to endure.

For much of modern American history, politics operated quietly in the background of daily life. Elections mattered. Laws changed. Administrations came and went. Yet the underlying assumption remained that institutions would hold. Contracts would be honored. Rights would persist. Systems might be inefficient, but they would function. For most citizens, politics was something to follow, debate, even argue about—but rarely something that directly shaped where they could live, how they accessed healthcare, or whether their savings were secure.

That era has ended.

Over the past decade, politics has moved from background to foreground, from context to condition. It now intrudes on decisions once governed primarily by lifestyle or economics. For Americans contemplating life abroad, this shift is impossible to ignore. Politics no longer merely colors experience; it defines the framework within which experience unfolds.

At first glance, this can feel counterintuitive. When people imagine moving overseas, their thoughts naturally drift toward food, scenery, climate, or affordability. They picture cafés, coastlines, walkable streets, and slower rhythms of life. Parliamentary systems and visa regulations rarely feature in those early fantasies. Yet the longer one looks, the clearer it becomes that politics is the invisible hand shaping every practical outcome of expatriation.

Politics decides who gets in, who gets to stay, and under what conditions. It determines whether residency pathways are stable or subject to sudden reversal. It governs taxation, healthcare access, property ownership, and legal protection. It defines whether institutions are boring and functional or volatile and arbitrary.

In an unsettled world, politics is no longer something to tolerate passively. It is something to assess deliberately.

The Architecture of Daily Life

Politics is often misunderstood as spectacle—elections, scandals, speeches, and protests. But for someone choosing where to live, politics is better understood as architecture. It is the structural framework beneath daily life, shaping how smoothly—or how precariously—that life unfolds.

Immigration policy offers the clearest example. A country's political posture toward migrants determines whether expatriation is feasible at all. Some governments actively court newcomers, recognizing demographic decline or the economic value of foreign residents. Others tolerate them conditionally, subject to shifting quotas, tightening rules, or public backlash. Still others view outsiders with suspicion, erecting bureaucratic barriers designed less to regulate migration than to discourage it.

These distinctions are not abstract. They determine whether a retiree can plan with confidence, whether a remote worker can remain legally employed, and whether a family can put down roots without fear of disruption. A welcoming policy can feel like an open door; a hostile one can turn daily life into a constant negotiation with bureaucracy.

Taxation tells a similar story. Whether foreign income is taxed favorably, whether pensions are protected from double taxation, whether treaties exist to prevent financial limbo—all of these are political decisions that shape not just the affordability of a place, but its long-term viability. Two countries with similar costs of living can feel radically different once tax policy is applied.

Healthcare, too, is inseparable from politics. In some nations, access to public healthcare follows residency almost automatically, reflecting a political commitment to universality. In others, healthcare remains fragmented, privatized, or tied to employment, leaving expatriates exposed to high costs and uneven coverage. These systems are not accidents. They are the result of decades of political choice.

Even the most mundane aspects of daily life—reliable public transportation, functional internet, responsive municipal services—are political outcomes. They reflect priorities set, budgets passed, and institutions maintained over time. Where governance is competent, life feels smoother. Where it is dysfunctional, friction accumulates everywhere.

Stability Versus Volatility

What many expatriates ultimately seek is not ideological alignment, but stability. Stability does not mean stasis: it means predictability—knowing that rules will not change overnight, that institutions will not be arbitrarily weaponized, that disputes will be resolved through process rather than power.

This is why political volatility matters more than political leaning. A country may lean left or right, liberal or conservative, and still offer a stable environment if institutions are strong and norms are respected. Conversely, a country with appealing policies on paper can become unlivable if governance is erratic or authoritarian tendencies take hold.

For foreigners, volatility carries amplified risk. Citizens can vote, protest, or litigate from a position of belonging. Expatriates operate on permission. Their right to remain, work, own property, or access services can be altered by political shifts over which they have little influence.

This reality demands a different kind of attention—one must look beyond current leadership to underlying structures. How independent are the courts? How free is the press? How entrenched are democratic norms? How resilient are institutions during a crisis?

Countries with strong answers to these questions tend to absorb shocks without radical disruption. Those without them may lurch from one crisis to the next, leaving residents—especially foreign ones—exposed.

The American Context: Pressure From Within

Before turning outward, it is necessary to acknowledge the internal forces pushing many Americans to reconsider their place in the world.

Politics in the United States has undergone a profound transformation—not merely in policy outcomes, but in tone, trust, and emotional impact. Congressional gridlock has become chronic. Polarization has deepened to the point where compromise is treated as betrayal. Public discourse is saturated with outrage, suspicion, and fear.

This environment exacts a psychological toll. Politics is no longer something one checks periodically; it permeates daily life through media, social interaction, and even family relationships. For many, it feels inescapable.

High-profile events— contested elections, institutional breakdowns, the reversal of long-standing legal precedents, uneven responses to national crises—have accelerated a sense of unease. Trust in institutions has eroded. Confidence in continuity has weakened. The assumption that the system will reliably self-correct no longer feels universally convincing.

Importantly, this disillusionment crosses ideological lines. Fatigue with dysfunction is widespread. For some, it inspires renewed engagement. For others, it prompts a quieter question: What might life feel like elsewhere?

Politics as a Long-Term Variable

One of the most common mistakes prospective expatriates make is evaluating politics as a snapshot rather than a trajectory. A country may look attractive today while moving toward instability. Another may appear bureaucratic or dull while quietly strengthening democratic norms and institutional capacity.

Understanding this requires patience and discipline. It means looking beyond headlines to patterns—how power transfers occur, how dissent is handled, how outsiders are treated during moments of stress.

Expatriation is rarely reversible without cost. It involves emotional investment, financial commitment, and often irreversible change. Choosing a politically stable environment increases the likelihood that those investments will be protected.

Su's story is an extreme example, but not an outdated one. Politics has always shaped who can stay, who must leave, and who thrives. What has changed is how visible that influence has become.

Politics may not be the reason people first dream of life abroad. But in the world as it now exists, it is often the reason they succeed—or fail—once they arrive.

Part II: Stability, Drift, and the Price of Uncertainty

Once politics is understood as infrastructure rather than theater, the global landscape comes into sharper focus. Countries are no longer judged simply by whether their governments lean left or right, progressive or conservative, but by the durability of their political systems. For expatriates, this durability is not a philosophical preference. It is a practical necessity.

In recent years, political instability has become one of the defining features of the global order. Democratic backsliding, populist movements, and the concentration of executive power have appeared in regions once assumed to be immune. At the same time, a smaller number of countries have quietly strengthened institutions, reinforced transparency, and prioritized long-term governance over short-term gain.

The divergence between these paths is widening. And for those considering life abroad, it has never mattered more which direction a country is moving.

Predictability Over Alignment

Many Americans approach international politics through the lens of ideology. They ask whether a country's values align with their own, whether policies feel familiar or foreign, whether cultural norms mirror those of home. While these questions are understandable, they often miss the more important issue: predictability.

A predictable political system allows people to plan. It creates an environment where laws change gradually, where policy shifts are signaled in advance, where institutions absorb conflict rather than amplifying it. Even when decisions are unpopular, they follow processes that are recognizable and consistent.

For expatriates, predictability is a form of protection. It reduces the risk that visas will be revoked arbitrarily, that tax rules will change retroactively, that property rights will be challenged without recourse. It provides confidence that disputes will be resolved through courts rather than connections, through rules rather than power.

This is why countries with very different ideological orientations can feel equally livable if their institutions are strong. It is also why countries with appealing rhetoric can feel precarious if governance is erratic.

The Global Rise of Populism

One of the most significant political trends of the past decade has been the rise of populism—movements that frame politics as a struggle between "the people" and perceived elites, often accompanied by skepticism toward institutions, media, and minority protections.

Populism does not always lead to authoritarianism. In some cases, it serves as a corrective, highlighting real grievances and forcing overdue reforms. In others, however, it becomes a vehicle for consolidating power, weakening checks and balances, and marginalizing dissent.

For expatriates, populism carries particular risks. Foreign residents are easy symbols in nationalist narratives. They can be portrayed as beneficiaries of unfair advantage, cultural outsiders, or economic competitors. Even when policies are not explicitly hostile, the tone of public discourse can shift in ways that make life less welcoming, more uncertain.

This dynamic has played out repeatedly. Immigration programs that were once celebrated become politically vulnerable. Residency pathways are tightened or closed. Tax incentives are withdrawn. Bureaucratic hurdles multiply. What was once a clear path forward becomes a maze.

When considering a move abroad, populism should automatically disqualify a country, but political mood matters. A society under strain may tolerate foreigners during prosperity and turn inward during crisis.

Authoritarian Drift and Its Consequences

More concerning than populism alone is authoritarian drift—the gradual erosion of democratic norms and institutional independence. This process is often incremental, unfolding over years rather than months. Courts are politicized. Media outlets are pressured or captured. Civil society organizations are constrained. Elections continue, but the playing field tilts.

Countries experiencing this trajectory often remain attractive in early stages. From the outside, systems can appear stable. Costs are low. Culture is rich. Infrastructure may be modern. Growth may even continue for a time. But beneath the surface, risk accumulates.

For expatriates, authoritarian drift creates a particularly vulnerable position, and the long-term trajectory matters more than the present moment. Legal protections weaken. Arbitrary enforcement becomes more common. Exit becomes harder. In extreme cases, capital controls or travel restrictions trap residents who assumed mobility would always be available.

Living well in such environments often requires proximity to power or a willingness to accept uncertainty as a constant. For those seeking stability rather than adventure, this is a significant trade-off.

The Quiet Strength of Functional Democracies

Against this backdrop, a subset of countries stands out not for ideological purity, but for institutional competence. These are places where democratic processes are relatively boring, where power changes hands peacefully, where scandals lead to reform rather than rupture.

Countries such as Portugal, Finland, Canada, New Zealand, and Uruguay are often cited in this category—not because they are perfect, but because they are predictable. Governance is procedural. Corruption is limited. Courts are independent. Media is pluralistic.

For expatriates, this predictability translates into confidence. Residency programs may evolve, but they rarely disappear overnight. Tax systems may be complex, but they are transparent. Healthcare and education function as expected. Political disputes occur, but they do not dominate daily life.

This does not mean these societies are immune to global pressures. Economic shocks, migration debates, and cultural tensions exist everywhere. The difference lies in how they are managed. In functional democracies, stress tends to produce adjustment rather than breakdown.

The Expat's Asymmetry

One of the most important realities for expatriates is asymmetry. Citizens and non-citizens experience politics differently.

Citizens have voice. They vote. They organize. They can influence outcomes, even marginally. Expatriates, by contrast, live under rules they did not help create and may not be able to change. Their relationship to the state is conditional.

This asymmetry makes political stability more important, not less. A citizen may tolerate volatility as the price of participation. An expatriate bears volatility without representation.

Understanding this distinction helps explain why some destinations feel comfortable for tourists but stressful for residents. A short stay may obscure bureaucratic friction, legal ambiguity, or social tension that becomes obvious over time.

It also explains why expatriates often gravitate toward countries with strong rule of law, even if those countries feel less exciting. Predictability is easier to appreciate when one lacks political leverage.

Crisis as a Revealer

Political systems are best evaluated not during calm, but during crisis. How did a country respond to the pandemic? To economic shock? To refugee inflows? To natural disasters? Did institutions coordinate effectively? Were policies communicated clearly? Were rights respected? Did trust increase or erode?

These moments reveal the true character of governance. Some countries emerged from recent crises with strengthened institutions and renewed public confidence. Others exposed deep fractures, opportunism, or incompetence.

For those considering expatriation, these recent stress tests provide valuable data.

Choosing Calm Over Drama

One of the least discussed benefits of political stability is psychological. Living in a country where politics does not dominate the emotional landscape can be profoundly calming.

This does not mean disengagement. It means proportion. Politics matters, but it does not consume. News cycles are shorter. Disagreements are less apocalyptic. Governance feels like administration rather than spectacle.

For many expatriates, this shift alone justifies the move. The absence of constant political drama frees attention for work, relationships, and personal growth. Life feels less adversarial.

This calm is not accidental. It is the product of systems designed to lower stakes, diffuse power, and manage conflict incrementally.

Reading the Direction of Travel

Expatriation is not a bet on a moment; it is a bet on a trajectory.Ultimately, the most important political question is not, "What is this country like today?" but, "Where is it headed?"

A country moving toward greater transparency, institutional independence, and inclusion may be worth patience, even if it is imperfect now. A country moving in the opposite direction may warrant caution, regardless of present advantages.

Let's turn now from analysis to application—how expatriates can assess political risk, protect themselves legally and financially, and build lives that remain flexible even when systems change.

Part III: Living Well Inside Other People's Systems

At some point, every successful expatriate arrives at the same realization: you are not moving to escape politics, you are moving to live inside a different political system—and to do so without being crushed by it.

This recognition marks a shift from romantic exploration to mature planning. It replaces the question, "Do I like this country?" with a more useful one: "Can I live here securely over time, even when conditions change?"

Politics, after all, does not only reveal itself in elections or protests. It reveals itself in paperwork, in courtrooms, in hospitals, in tax offices, and in moments of crisis. For foreigners, these encounters carry extra weight, as foreigners do not have the luxury of misunderstanding the system they inhabit.

Reading Political Risk Like a Resident

The most common mistake expatriates make is assuming that political risk is something dramatic and sudden. In reality, it is usually procedural and incremental.

Residency rules tighten quietly. Tax reporting requirements expand. Banking compliance grows more intrusive. Foreign ownership laws are adjusted. None of these changes make headlines. Yet each one can materially alter the feasibility of staying.

The expatriate who thrives long-term learns to read political risk the way locals do—not through headlines, but through patterns. How often do laws change? How much discretion do bureaucrats have? Are rules enforced uniformly, or selectively? Does the system reward compliance, or connections?

In countries with strong institutions, rules may be complex, but consistent. In weaker systems, rules may appear simple but are applied unpredictably. This distinction matters far more than the letter of the law.

A useful heuristic is to observe how a country treats its own citizens when systems are stressed. Are benefits withdrawn arbitrarily? Are contracts rewritten retroactively? Are courts bypassed? If citizens are vulnerable, foreigners will be more so.

Legal Status as Political Insulation

Nothing matters more politically than legal status. Tourists live in a fantasy; residents live in reality.

Tourist visas offer flexibility but no protection. They are easily revoked, strictly limited, and provide no access to public systems. They are useful for exploration, but dangerous for planning.

Residency, by contrast, creates a legal relationship with the state. It defines rights and obligations. It provides access to healthcare, banking, housing, and—in some cases—social services. It also offers predictability.

The strength of that predictability depends on the security of the residency pathway. Some countries offer renewable permits with clear criteria and transparent processes. Others retain broad discretion, allowing authorities to deny renewals without explanation.

This distinction is political. It reflects how a country views foreigners—not merely as guests, but as stakeholders.

Expatriates seeking long-term stability should prioritize jurisdictions where residency is governed by statute rather than whim, where renewals are routine rather than adversarial, and where pathways to permanence exist even if citizenship is not desired.

Taxes, Transparency, and Trust

Tax systems are another point where politics becomes personal. High taxes are not necessarily a problem. Unpredictable taxes are.

In well-governed countries, tax obligations are clear, enforcement is consistent, and treaties reduce the risk of double taxation. Even when the burden is substantial, it is at least legible.

In less stable environments, tax policy can change suddenly, enforcement may be arbitrary, and foreigners may be targeted as revenue sources during fiscal stress. This creates anxiety and discourages long-term commitment.

For Americans, who already face the complexity of worldwide taxation, clarity matters. The ability to plan across borders—to understand how income, pensions, and investments will be treated—is inseparable from political stability.

This is why many expatriates gravitate toward countries with boring tax systems. They may not be optimized for avoidance, but they are optimized for compliance without fear.

Healthcare as a Political Promise

Healthcare reveals the moral core of a political system. It reflects how a society balances individual responsibility and collective care.

For expatriates, healthcare policy is not an abstract debate. It determines whether you will be treated as a human being or a customer in moments of vulnerability.

In countries where healthcare is universal and tied to residency, expatriates often experience a profound sense of relief. The anxiety of catastrophic expense disappears. Preventive care becomes routine. Aging feels less frightening.

In systems where healthcare is privatized or fragmented, access can be inconsistent, especially for foreigners. Coverage gaps, preexisting condition exclusions, and high out-of-pocket costs introduce uncertainty into long-term planning.

These outcomes are political, the result of choices made over decades. They tend to be stable—until they are not. Evaluating healthcare policy, therefore, requires the same long view as evaluating climate or economics. What has this country committed to? How well has it honored that commitment over time?

Social Climate and Informal Politics

Politics does not end at the border of formal institutions. It permeates social norms, attitudes, and everyday interactions.

For members of minority groups—whether defined by race, religion, gender identity, or sexual orientation—this informal politics matters enormously. Laws may promise protection, but social acceptance determines whether life feels safe or exhausting.

Countries differ widely in this regard. Some offer strong legal protections paired with cultural openness. Others offer formal rights but uneven enforcement. Still others impose explicit restrictions.

For expatriates, especially those visible as outsiders, this social climate shapes daily life more than politics ever could. It affects whether neighbors are welcoming, whether bureaucracy is cooperative, whether conflicts escalate or resolve quietly.

Understanding this dimension requires humility and observation. It cannot be gleaned from statistics alone.

Exit as a Feature, not a Failure

One of the most important political advantages expatriates can preserve is the ability to leave.

This does not mean living with one foot out the door. It means structuring life in a way that preserves mobility. Maintaining valid travel documents. Avoiding entanglements that are difficult to unwind. Keeping financial access outside the host country. Retaining legal ties elsewhere. Having an exit strategy is not pessimism. It is prudence.

History is full of examples where systems changed faster than residents expected. Borders closed. Capital controls were imposed. Residency rules tightened. Those with options adapted. Those without endured.

Expatriation should increase freedom, not reduce it. The goal is not to trade one rigid system for another, but to inhabit systems lightly enough to move when necessary.

Choosing Political Fit

Ultimately, the politics of place is about fit. Not perfection or agreement, but fit.

Some people thrive in highly structured societies with clear rules and high expectations; others prefer flexibility and informality. Some value social cohesion; others value autonomy. Some are comfortable navigating ambiguity; others find it draining.

Political fit aligns with temperament as much as ideology. The right system supports your way of living rather than constantly challenging it.

For many Americans, this realization is liberating. It reframes expatriation not as rejection of home, but as selection of context, a choice about where your energy is best spent.

Where This Leaves Us

Climate change constrains the physical world. The global economy constrains opportunity. Politics constrains possibility.

Together, they shape the terrain of modern life. None can be ignored without consequence.

The rise in American expatriation is not a fad. It is a rational response to a world in flux, reflecting a growing awareness that quality of life depends not just on personal effort, but on the systems within which effort is rewarded or frustrated.

Choosing where to live has become one of the most consequential decisions a person can make. It requires attention to forces once taken for granted.

The reward for that attention can be extraordinary: a life lived with less friction, greater security, and a sense that politics, while always present, no longer dominates the emotional or practical landscape.

In the chapters ahead, we will turn to the mechanics of making such a move—residency pathways, legal status, healthcare access, and financial planning—building on the understanding that where you live is not just a place on a map, but a complex ecosystem you inhabit every day.

Chapter 4

DOLLARS, DOCUMENTS & DOUBLE TAXATION

THE FINANCIAL REALITY OF EXPATRIATION

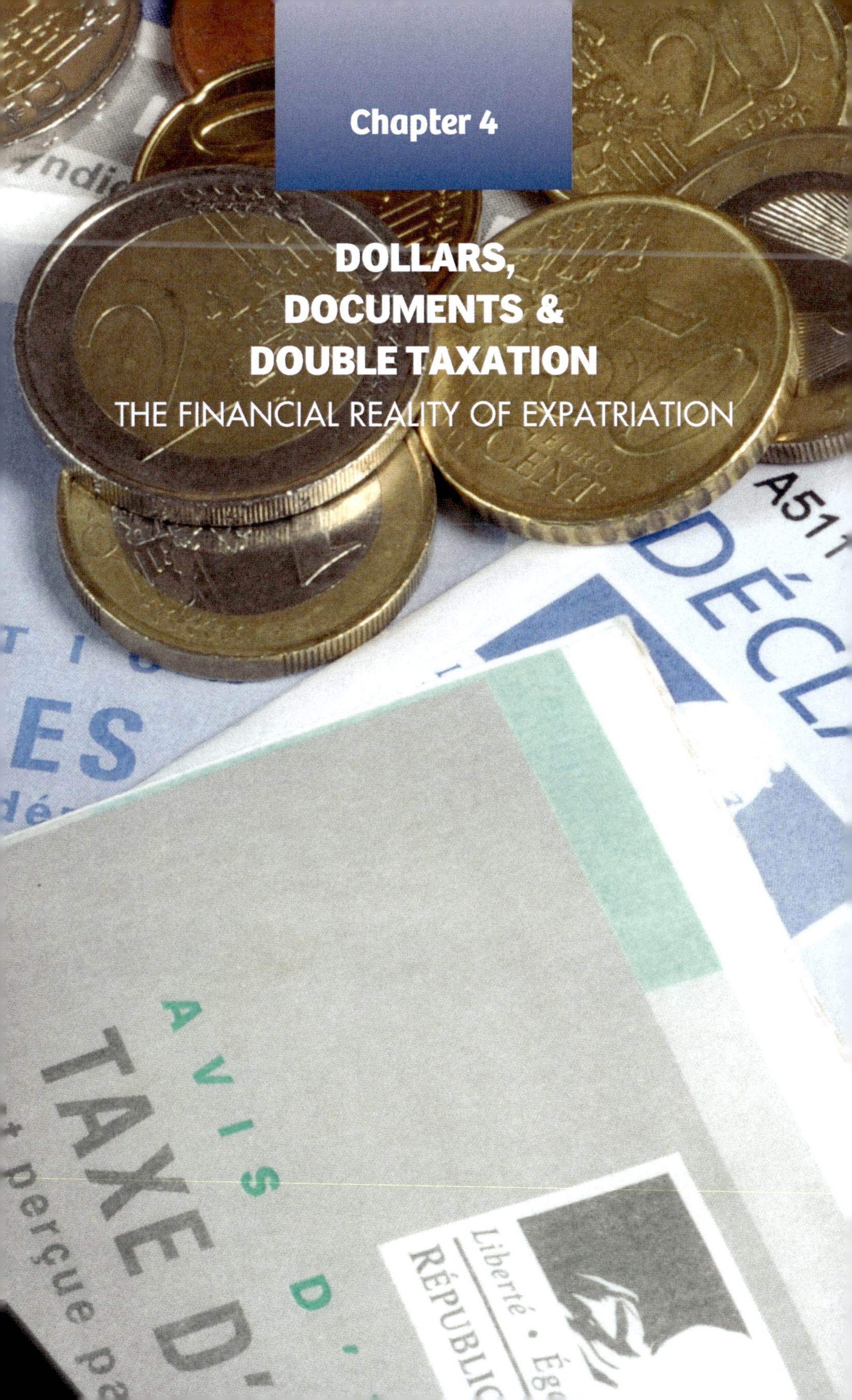

Part I: The Paper Trail That Follows You

David and April were a young married couple living in San Francisco's Mission District, drawn—as many are—to a life that felt broader than one city or one country. They spent long stretches of time in Mexico, particularly on the outskirts of Guadalajara, where they rented half of a historic two-family home. They were not Hispanic, but both spoke excellent Spanish. They knew the culture well enough to feel comfortable, confident—even settled.

After a couple of years of renting, they decided to buy the place. Or more precisely, they decided to buy their half of it. That was when the nightmare began.

The purchase itself seemed straightforward: a price was negotiated, funds were transferred and converted into pesos, contracts were signed. On paper, everything appeared complete. But because the property was jointly owned with another family, ownership did not resolve cleanly. The documentation multiplied. The explanations shifted. Each step forward introduced new conditions, new approvals, new interpretations of what "ownership" actually meant.

They could stay in the house. They lived there. They paid for it. But to this day, it is unclear whether they hold a truly clear title.

Nothing about their experience involved fraud or bad faith. The problem was structural. They had stepped into a legal and financial system that operated under different assumptions, different norms, and different definitions of finality. What they thought was a transaction turned out to be an ongoing negotiation between registries, jurisdictions, and interpretations that did not align neatly with their expectations—or with one another.

David and April's story is not unusual. Their experience was not the result of naïveté or poor judgment, but of a deeper mismatch between expectations formed in one legal culture and realities enforced in another—a mismatch that defines the financial side of expatriation far more often than people expect.

When Americans imagine life abroad, they tend to picture historic streets, slower mornings, better food, lower costs, and a sense of distance from the noise and pressure of home. What they rarely picture is paperwork. Not the occasional form or signature, but a permanent financial trail that follows them across borders, linking bank accounts, tax authorities, immigration offices, and legal systems that were never designed to work seamlessly together.

Yet this paper trail is not a nuisance. It is the system. Relocating abroad is not merely a change of scenery. It is an entry into a new financial and legal ecosystem that operates under different assumptions, rules, and risks.

For Americans, that transition is uniquely complex. Unlike almost every other nationality, U.S. citizens do not leave their tax obligations behind when they leave the country: they carry them for life.

This fact reshapes the expatriation experience more than climate, culture, or cost of living ever could. It means that moving abroad is not just a lifestyle decision. It is a financial transformation—one that demands planning, discipline, and a willingness to confront complexity head-on.

Without preparation, the consequences can be severe. Double taxation, frozen bank accounts, denied visas, penalties for missed filings, and long-term erosion of retirement security are common outcomes for people who move first and plan later.

The American Exception

Most countries tax people based on residence. If you move to Spain, Spanish tax law governs your income. If you live in Portugal, Portuguese rules apply. Your prior citizenship may matter for visas, but not for taxation. Once you leave, the financial relationship largely ends.

The United States is different.

The U.S. taxes its citizens on worldwide income, regardless of where they live, work, or retire. Whether you earn your income in New York, Lisbon, or Bangkok, the IRS expects a return every year. All income must be reported. All qualifying foreign accounts must be disclosed. Compliance is not optional, and penalties for failure can be catastrophic.

This reality surprises many Americans, even sophisticated ones. They assume that once they pay taxes abroad, their obligations at home must diminish. In fact, the opposite is often true. Living abroad introduces new reporting requirements layered on top of existing ones, expanding both complexity and risk.

Consider the retiree who relocates to France with a U.S. pension and Social Security income. Her checks are deposited into an American bank account and taxed by the United States. France, however, views her as a tax resident and claims the right to tax that same income. Without careful use of the U.S.-France tax treaty, she can easily pay twice. If her tax preparer is unfamiliar with cross-border rules—and many are—the error may go unnoticed for years.

Or consider the entrepreneur working remotely from Spain. His U.S. income satisfies Spanish visa requirements, but once residency is established, Spain considers him a tax resident as well. His salary becomes subject to Spanish taxation, while the IRS still requires full reporting. Add in business income, foreign bank accounts, and reporting obligations like FBAR (Foreign Bank and Financial Accounts), and the margin for error narrows quickly.

Ignorance does not soften enforcement. It amplifies penalties.

Compliance Is Not Strategy

One of the most dangerous misconceptions about expatriation is the belief that compliance alone is sufficient. Filing the required forms, paying what appears to be owed, and hoping for the best may keep you out of immediate trouble, but it rarely produces optimal outcomes.

Compliance answers the question, "Am I legal?" Strategy answers a more important question: "Am I protected?"

The distinction matters because international financial systems do not coordinate automatically. Tax authorities operate independently. Immigration officials focus on income sufficiency, not tax efficiency. Banks respond to regulatory risk, not customer convenience. Each system sees only its own mandate, and expatriates sit at the intersection. This is where problems emerge.

A residency application may require proof of income that is technically sufficient but structured in a way that triggers unnecessary taxation. A bank account opened for convenience may cross reporting thresholds without the account holder realizing it. A currency transfer meant to simplify life may temporarily push balances above limits that trigger severe penalties if not disclosed.

None of this reflects wrongdoing. It reflects fragmentation.

The Price of Residency

Most countries that welcome foreign residents require proof of financial self-sufficiency. This requirement is not symbolic: it is central to immigration policy. Governments want assurance that newcomers will not strain public systems or become economically vulnerable.

What counts as sufficient income varies widely. Some countries emphasize passive income, others accept employment income, and still others require funds to be held locally. Documentation must often be precise, current, and translated or notarized. Immigration authorities rarely make exceptions, and appeals are limited.

For Americans accustomed to flexible systems, this rigidity can be jarring. A portfolio that easily supports life may not satisfy visa criteria if income streams are irregular or poorly documented. Assets that are liquid in practice may not be recognized if held in the "wrong" accounts.

This is where financial planning intersects directly with legal status. The way income is structured, reported, and presented can determine whether residency is granted or denied. The difference between success and failure is often not wealth, but preparation.

Money in Motion

Once residency is secured, the financial challenges evolve rather than disappear. Living abroad introduces currency risk, banking friction, and new exposure to inflation dynamics that differ from those in the United States.

Americans often assume that a lower cost of living guarantees long-term affordability. In reality, exchange rates and local inflation can quietly erode purchasing power. A retirement income that feels generous in year one may feel tight in year five if the dollar weakens or local prices rise faster than expected.

At the same time, banking abroad as a U.S. citizen introduces unique complications. Foreign banks face strict reporting requirements under U.S. law, and some choose not to serve Americans at all. Accounts may be denied, closed, or limited. U.S. banks, meanwhile, may flag foreign activity as suspicious, freezing accounts without warning.

This friction is not personal. It is regulatory. But its impact is deeply personal.

The expatriate who plans well anticipates these constraints. Accounts are structured intentionally. Transfers are timed and documented. Currency exposure is managed rather than ignored. Financial systems are designed to function smoothly across borders rather than patched together reactively.

The Cost of Getting It Wrong

What makes financial planning abroad unforgiving is not the complexity itself, but the asymmetry of consequences. A missed filing can generate penalties far exceeding the underlying balance. A misapplied treaty can result in years of unnecessary taxation. A frozen account can leave someone temporarily unable to access funds in a foreign country.

These outcomes often occur quietly, without drama, until they suddenly demand attention.

The stories shared later in this chapter are not exceptional. They are representative. They illustrate how easily well-intentioned Americans can stumble into financial traps simply by assuming that systems will work together automatically.

A New Definition of Preparedness

We have explored how climate, economics, and politics shape the feasibility of life abroad. Finance is where those forces converge. It is the layer that translates abstract risk into concrete consequence.

Preparedness, in this context, does not mean mastering tax codes or memorizing visa requirements. It means recognizing that expatriation requires a different level of intentionality. It means assembling expertise early rather than repairing damage later. It means understanding that the freedom to live abroad rests on a foundation of compliance, structure, and foresight.

The good news is that this foundation can be built. With the right planning, expatriation can reduce financial stress rather than increase it. It can preserve wealth rather than expose it. It can create flexibility rather than constraint. But only if the paperwork is treated not as an afterthought, but as the architecture that supports the life you are trying to build.

Part II: Living Inside Two Financial Systems at Once

Once the initial move is complete and residency is secured, many Americans expect the financial complexity of expatriation to settle down. The opposite is usually true. The first year abroad often feels manageable, even deceptively simple. Income continues to arrive. Bills get paid. Life resumes. It is only with time that the deeper mechanics reveal themselves, as the reality of living inside two financial systems at once becomes unavoidable.

This duality defines the American expatriate experience. You are never fully "out" of the U.S. system, no matter how long you live elsewhere. At the same time, your host country increasingly asserts its own claims on your income, your assets, your healthcare, and your future. The challenge is not choosing one system over the other, but learning how to exist between them without being pulled apart.

The Annual Ritual: U.S. Taxes from Abroad

Every year, the American expatriate returns—on paper—to the United States. A federal tax return must be filed, reporting worldwide income in full. This includes wages, pensions, business income, rental income, dividends, and interest, regardless of where those earnings were generated or where the accounts are held.

There are mechanisms designed to prevent double taxation, but they are neither automatic nor intuitive. The Foreign Earned Income Exclusion allows qualifying individuals to exclude a portion of foreign earned income if they meet residency or physical presence tests. The Foreign Tax Credit allows U.S. taxpayers to offset U.S. tax liability with taxes paid to a foreign government. Tax treaties can allocate taxing rights between countries, but each treaty is different, and many contain traps for the unwary.

What makes this process especially treacherous is that these tools are mutually exclusive in certain contexts. Choosing the wrong approach in one year can limit options in future years. Misclassifying income can invalidate exclusions. Failing to coordinate U.S. and foreign filings can produce phantom tax liabilities that exist only because forms were mismatched.

The system assumes competence. It does not forgive confusion.

When Residency Changes Everything

The moment an American becomes a tax resident of another country, the financial equation shifts. Residency, not citizenship, determines local tax obligations. Once established, the host country typically claims the right to tax global income, just as the United States does. This overlap is where double taxation risk peaks.

A digital worker earning U.S. wages while living in Spain may discover that Spanish tax rates exceed those at home. A retiree drawing from a U.S. pension may find that the host country taxes distributions differently, or at different times, than the IRS. Investment income that is tax-efficient in the United States may be treated harshly abroad, particularly if the host country does not recognize certain tax-deferred structures.

These outcomes are not punishments. They are the result of systems built independently, each optimized for its own citizens. The expatriate who does not anticipate this overlap often learns the hard way that residency is not merely permission to stay. It is a financial turning point.

Retirement Income in a Foreign Context

For many Americans, retirement income is the anchor that makes expatriation possible. Pensions, Social Security, and retirement accounts provide predictable cash flow and satisfy visa requirements in many countries. But once abroad, these income streams are treated differently.

Social Security can usually be collected overseas, but how it is taxed varies widely. Some countries exempt it entirely. Others treat it as ordinary income. Some tax it only if remitted locally. These distinctions can dramatically alter net income.

Retirement accounts introduce even greater complexity. Withdrawals from IRAs and 401(k)s remain taxable in the United States, but the host country may also claim a share. Some treaties allocate taxing rights clearly; others are silent or ambiguous. Required minimum distributions may also be recognized differently, creating timing mismatches that complicate planning.

What worked domestically may no longer be optimal. Distribution strategies may need adjustment. Account sequencing matters. In some cases, preemptive restructuring—while still in the United States—can simplify life later. Once abroad, options narrow. The expatriate who treats retirement planning as static risks locking in inefficiencies that persist for decades.

Currency: The Silent Variable

Currency risk is one of the most underestimated forces in expatriate life. It operates quietly, without paperwork or deadlines, yet its cumulative effect can rival that of taxation.

When income and expenses are denominated in different currencies, volatility becomes part of daily life. A strengthening local currency can erode purchasing power; a weakening one can inflate costs for imported goods or international travel. Over time, these shifts reshape budgets in ways that feel arbitrary and unfair.

The temptation is to ignore currency risk, assuming that fluctuations will "even out." Sometimes they do. Often they do not.

Living abroad requires accepting that currency is not neutral. It is an active participant in your financial life. Managing exposure—through diversification, timing, and account structure—becomes part of long-term stability.

This does not mean speculating on exchange rates, but acknowledging that where money is held, in what currency, and for what purpose matters.

Banking Friction and Regulatory Reality

Banking abroad as an American introduces a layer of friction that many do not anticipate. U.S. regulations aimed at combating tax evasion impose heavy compliance burdens on foreign financial institutions. Some respond by limiting services to U.S. citizens. Others impose additional documentation requirements. Accounts may be opened reluctantly, monitored closely, or closed abruptly.

At the same time, U.S. banks may flag foreign activity as suspicious, particularly if customers fail to update residency information. Account freezes are not uncommon. Transfers may be delayed. Access to funds can be disrupted at precisely the wrong moment.

These frictions are manageable, but only if anticipated. Communication matters. Documentation matters. Choosing institutions experienced with cross-border clients matters.

The expatriate who assumes that banking will "just work" often discovers that it does work—until it doesn't.

Healthcare as a Financial System

Healthcare is often cited as a benefit of living abroad, and in many cases, it is. Costs are lower. Access is broader. Outcomes are comparable or better. But healthcare is also a financial system governed by politics, insurance markets, and residency status.

Medicare does not travel. Private international insurance is often required, at least initially. Public healthcare may become available only after residency is established, and even then, coverage levels vary.

Premiums rise with age. Coverage terms change. Some systems require co-payments or supplemental insurance. Emergency evacuation coverage may be prudent, especially for those living in remote areas or traveling frequently.

Underestimating healthcare costs can derail an otherwise sound plan. Overestimating them can unnecessarily constrain lifestyle. Accurate budgeting requires understanding not just prices, but eligibility, timing, and coverage gaps.

Healthcare planning abroad is not about finding the cheapest option. It is about ensuring continuity of care without financial shock.

The Compounding Effect

What makes expatriate finance challenging is not any single factor, but the way various components interact. Taxes influence cash flow. Cash flow affects visa renewals. Currency shifts alter purchasing power. Healthcare costs change with age. Banking regulations evolve. Political decisions reshape rules.

These forces compound over time. Small inefficiencies become significant. Minor oversights accumulate. What felt manageable in the first year can become burdensome by the fifth.

This is why expatriation cannot be treated as a one-time transaction. It is an ongoing relationship with multiple systems that evolve independently. Staying ahead requires attention, adjustment, and, often, professional guidance.

Part III: Making It Durable

The financial challenges of expatriation rarely arrive all at once. They unfold over time, often quietly, as life settles into routine and attention shifts elsewhere. This gradualism is precisely what makes them dangerous. By the time problems surface, they are no longer theoretical—they are expensive, stressful, and difficult to unwind.

The Americans who succeed abroad over the long term are not the ones who find clever loopholes or exploit temporary incentives. They are the ones who build financial systems designed to endure change. They plan not for best-case scenarios, but for the messy middle years when currencies fluctuate, rules evolve, and personal circumstances shift.

Durability, not cleverness, is the goal.

When Reality Arrives: Three Lives Abroad

Maria moved to central Mexico after retiring from a long career in California. San Miguel de Allende offered beauty, culture, and an active expatriate community. Her budget seemed generous at first. Her U.S. Social Security and modest pension easily covered rent, food, and healthcare, and the lower cost of living felt like a windfall.

The first disruption came quietly. Her U.S. bank flagged repeated logins from Mexico and temporarily froze her account. Resolving the issue took weeks of calls and documentation. Soon after, she transferred funds to a local Mexican account to place a deposit on a rental property. The balance exceeded reporting thresholds briefly—just long enough to trigger a missed FBAR filing. The penalty notice that followed was nearly as large as the account itself.

Over time, the peso strengthened against the dollar. Her rent increased in real terms. Healthcare costs, still affordable, rose faster than expected as private insurance premiums adjusted for age. What had felt effortless in year one became increasingly constrained by year three.

Maria did not make reckless choices. She made ordinary ones without understanding how systems would interact. With proper planning, each issue could have been mitigated. Without it, they compounded.

David's story unfolded differently. In his mid-thirties, he left New York to work remotely from Barcelona. His employer remained U.S.-based and paid his income in dollars. He assumed this would keep his financial life simple.

Spain's digital nomad visa required proof of income, private health insurance, and a local bank account. Once residency was granted, Spain treated him as a tax resident. His U.S. salary became subject to Spanish tax rates, some higher than those at home. His U.S. accountant misapplied foreign tax credits, leaving him exposed to double taxation.

Banking proved unexpectedly difficult. Several Spanish banks declined to open accounts for him due to U.S. reporting requirements. Each delay affected his visa compliance. Instead of enjoying life in Barcelona, David spent his first year managing bureaucratic crises.

None of this was inevitable. With coordinated tax planning and banking support, his experience could have been smooth. Instead, it became reactive.

For the Johnson family, expatriation was a strategic choice. They moved from Chicago to Lisbon seeking stability, education, and a healthier pace of life for their children. Their income and savings easily qualified them for Portugal's residency program.

The surprises came later. International school tuition exceeded expectations. Currency fluctuations eroded the value of dollar-denominated savings. Their Portuguese accountant treated U.S. retirement accounts as taxable local investments, triggering unnecessary taxes. Their U.S. wills conflicted with Portuguese inheritance law, exposing their estate to avoidable taxation.

Each issue was solvable. Together, they revealed how financial planning abroad must account not just for income and expenses, but for law, language, and time.

Estate Planning: The Overlooked Risk

Estate planning abroad is not a luxury. It is a responsibility. Few expatriates think seriously about estate planning until forced to. This delay can be costly.

Inheritance laws vary dramatically across countries. Some follow common law traditions that emphasize testamentary freedom. Others impose forced heirship, dictating how assets must be distributed regardless of a will. Tax treatment differs as well. Assets may be taxed based on location, citizenship, residency, or the residency of heirs.

An American will drafted at home may not be recognized abroad. A trust that functions perfectly in the United States may be ignored or penalized elsewhere. Without coordination, heirs can find themselves navigating conflicting legal systems during moments of grief.

Even modest estates can face disproportionate exposure if improperly structured. Dual-jurisdiction planning is often necessary. Separate wills may be required. Asset location matters. Beneficiary designations must be reviewed in light of local law.

The Discipline of Ongoing Planning

What distinguishes successful expatriates from those who struggle is not intelligence or income, but discipline.

Cross-border financial planning is not a one-time project. It is an ongoing process that evolves as laws change, markets shift, and life unfolds. Residency requirements are updated, tax treaties are revised, healthcare systems adapt, and political decisions reshape incentives.

A sound plan anticipates this change. It builds in review cycles. And preserves flexibility by avoiding over-commitment to any single structure.

This is where professional guidance earns its value. A qualified cross-border advisor is not merely preparing returns or managing investments. They are monitoring exposure. They are adjusting strategies. They are ensuring that today's compliance does not become tomorrow's liability. The cost of this guidance is real. The cost of proceeding without it is often far higher.

Financial Freedom, Not Fantasy

Living abroad can deliver extraordinary rewards, including lower costs, better healthcare, richer daily experience, and a sense of agency reclaimed. But these rewards are sustained not by optimism, but by structure.

Financial freedom abroad is not the absence of rules; it is the mastery of them.

A new climate—environmental, economic, political—demands a new financial mindset. One that treats planning as infrastructure, not inconvenience. One that values durability over cleverness. One that accepts complexity as the price of expanded choice.

Expatriation is not about escaping responsibility, but assuming it deliberately, on your own terms, in a system you understand.

In the next chapter, we turn from money to movement—from financial architecture to legal pathways. Visas, residency, and the mechanics of staying put are where plans become real. Because a life abroad does not begin with a flight. It begins with permission.

Chapter 5

DIGITAL NOMADS

LIVING AND WORKING IN MOTION

Part I: Work Without a Fixed Address

My first real understanding of what would later be called digital nomadism did not come from theory, policy, or data. It came from lived experience—first through a friend, then through my own work, carried out far from any traditional office.

My friend and longtime sailboat crewmate Pete was, in many ways, the embodiment of the digital nomad long before the term became fashionable. American by birth but holding passports from both the U.S. and Italy, he lived in a modest apartment in Verona, Italy, building a software company that catered to the global hospitality industry. From northern Italy, he traveled constantly, moving across Europe, the Mediterranean, and beyond, growing his business client by client. Connectivity was improvised. He chased local SIM cards across borders to stay reachable and relied on Inmarsat satellite communications when terrestrial networks failed. On more than one occasion, he updated his company's software code while transiting the Mediterranean under sail.

Pete lived well. He lived internationally. And he built a thriving business from scratch without anchoring himself to any single city, office, or country. Geography did not define his career; it simply framed his days.

I was doing something similar in a very different profession.

While traveling extensively, I built and operated my financial services business across borders and time zones. One moment stands out as emblematic of how radically the relationship between work and place had changed: I once conducted a two-hour conference call with a client's attorney regarding a complex estate matter from the bow of an eighty-foot ketch in the South Pacific. We were en route from Fiji to Auckland, sailing through a hurricane, soaked by driving rain, using an old-generation Iridium satellite phone. The call proceeded uninterrupted. Advice was given. Decisions were made. The business of life continued.

Scenes like these would have been inconceivable in an earlier era.

For most of modern history, work anchored people to place. Careers grew around offices, cities, and commuting patterns. Where one lived was largely determined by where one was employed, and changing either usually required sacrificing the other. Geography was destiny.

That relationship has quietly broken.

In a world where connectivity matters more than proximity, a new class of globally mobile professionals has emerged—not as a novelty or subculture, but as a structural feature of the modern economy. These individuals are not drifters or dropouts. They work—often intensely—while living outside the country where their income originates. They earn, save, invest, and plan for the future, but they do so untethered to a single physical location.

They are commonly referred to as digital nomads, though many no longer identify with the term.

What began as a niche lifestyle—software developers working from cafés in Southeast Asia or freelance writers chasing low costs and adventure—has evolved into something far more mainstream. The pandemic accelerated a shift that was already underway, normalizing remote work across industries that once resisted it. Employers discovered that productivity did not depend on cubicles; employees discovered that their jobs did not require their zip codes.

For Americans in particular, this realization arrived amid compounding pressures. Housing costs soared. Urban stress intensified. Political polarization became exhausting. Climate risks grew harder to ignore. Against this backdrop, the ability to relocate without quitting work began to feel less like a novelty and more like a lifeline.

A New Kind of Mobility

The defining feature of today's digital nomad is not constant motion, but optionality. Many work full-time jobs for U.S.-based companies, paid in dollars, with benefits and long-term career trajectories. Others operate as freelancers, consultants, or business owners serving global clients. Some are transitioning professionals—experienced workers reshaping traditional careers into advisory or project-based roles that travel well.

What unites them is not age or industry, but a shared refusal to let geography dictate quality of life.

The popular stereotype of the twenty-something influencer hopping endlessly between tropical destinations captures only a narrow slice of reality. Increasingly, digital nomads are in their thirties, forties, and fifties. Some are single. Others have partners. A growing number have children. Many intend to remain abroad for years rather than months.

They are not chasing novelty for its own sake. They are seeking alignment—between work and life, income and cost, effort and reward.

For many, the initial motivation is pragmatic. A salary that barely sustains life in San Francisco can support a comfortable existence in Portugal. A remote role that feels constraining in New York can feel liberating when paired with walkable cities, access to nature, and functional public services. The same work, placed in a different context, produces a radically different lived experience.

Why the American Context Matters

Digital nomadism exists globally, but the American version carries particular weight. Americans bring with them a distinct mix of advantages and constraints. The advantage is income: U.S.-based salaries, consulting fees, and business revenues often travel well, especially in regions with lower costs of living. The constraint is obligation. As explored in the previous chapter, Americans remain subject to U.S. taxation and reporting regardless of where they live. This tension shapes the nomad experience.

The ability to earn globally while remaining legally and financially anchored to the United States creates both opportunity and complexity. It allows Americans to live well abroad without severing ties at home. It also demands careful planning to avoid legal, tax, and banking pitfalls that can quickly undermine the experience.

For digital nomads, expatriation is not an exit. It is a layering of systems. That layering becomes manageable only when approached deliberately. Those who treat digital nomadism as an extended vacation often encounter friction quickly. Those who treat it as a long-term lifestyle transition—one requiring structure, foresight, and professional discipline—are far more likely to succeed.

Part II: Choosing Place Without Being Trapped by It

Once work is liberated from geography, place becomes a variable rather than a constraint. This is the promise at the heart of digital nomadism: the ability to choose where to live based not on proximity to an office, but on the conditions that make daily life feel sustainable.

Yet this freedom is not infinite. It is shaped by infrastructure, law, cost, and culture. Over time, digital nomads learn that while they can live almost anywhere, only certain places truly support the rhythms of remote work over the long term.

The Geography of Function

Early in the nomad journey, destination choice is often aspirational or aesthetic. Beaches, historic centers, and Instagrammable views loom large. Over time, priorities shift. Reliable internet begins to matter more than scenery. Walkability replaces novelty. Proximity to healthcare, grocery stores, and co-working spaces becomes essential.

Successful digital nomads think in terms of function rather than fantasy. They ask how a place performs on an ordinary Tuesday, not how it looks in a photograph. Can meetings be taken without interruption? Is housing quiet enough for focused work? Does the city support routine rather than constant stimulation? These questions narrow the map.

Places that rise to the top tend to share certain characteristics. They have invested in digital infrastructure. They offer housing stock that accommodates longer stays rather than transient tourism. They maintain transport systems that allow daily life without a car. They have enough international presence to make integration feasible, but not so much that local character is erased.

In this sense, digital nomad hubs are less about spectacle and more about livability.

Europe's Quiet Magnetism

Europe has emerged as a focal point for American digital nomads, not because it is cheap in absolute terms, but because it offers a rare combination of infrastructure, culture, and legal clarity. Many European cities were built long before cars and sprawl, resulting in environments well-suited to pedestrian life and remote work.

Portugal illustrates this dynamic vividly. Its mild climate, safety, and modern infrastructure make it easy to settle into daily routines. Internet connectivity is fast and reliable. Healthcare is accessible. English is widely spoken. Cities like Lisbon and Porto offer urban energy, while coastal towns provide quieter alternatives without sacrificing connectivity.

What makes Portugal especially attractive is not any single feature, but the coherence of the system. Work, life, and logistics align with relatively little friction. This coherence explains why many digital nomads who arrive intending to stay for a few months end up renewing visas and establishing longer-term bases.

Spain follows a similar pattern, though with its own complexities. Cities like Barcelona and Valencia offer vibrant urban life paired with strong infrastructure and public services. Regional diversity allows nomads to experiment with different paces of life within the same country. The introduction of dedicated digital nomad visas has signaled official recognition of remote workers as legitimate residents rather than tolerated tourists.

Elsewhere in Europe, countries such as Estonia and Croatia have attracted nomads with explicit policy innovation. Estonia's embrace of digital governance reflects a broader national strategy, making it especially appealing to technologists and entrepreneurs. Croatia's visa regime offers clarity and, in some cases, favorable tax treatment for foreign income.

What unites these destinations is not uniformity, but intention. They have made conscious decisions to accommodate mobile professionals rather than leaving them to navigate legal gray zones indefinitely.

Beyond Europe's Core

While Europe draws many American nomads, it is not the only viable region. The Americas and parts of Asia continue to attract remote workers for different reasons.

Mexico remains popular, particularly for those who value proximity to the United States. Time zones align, flights are short, and cultural richness and affordability are combined with a large expatriate presence in cities like Mexico City, Guadalajara, and coastal regions. The ability to maintain U.S.-based work hours without extreme scheduling adjustments is a significant advantage.

Further south, countries like Costa Rica and Colombia offer appealing climates and growing digital communities. Costa Rica's political stability and environmental focus attract those seeking balance and predictability. Colombia's cities, particularly Medellín, have reinvented themselves as hubs for startups and remote work, offering mild climates and modern infrastructure.

In Southeast Asia, places like Thailand continue to draw nomads with low costs and established communities. Chiang Mai and Bangkok have long served as gateways, providing co-working spaces, reliable internet, and social networks built around remote work. Yet distance from U.S. time zones and evolving visa enforcement have pushed many nomads to move away from the hectic pace of U.S. life and adopt more deliberate, slower patterns of movement.

Destination choice is less about novelty than about sustainability. The longer one plans to stay, the more weight infrastructure and legality carry.

Visas: From Tolerance to Recognition

The most significant shift in digital nomadism over the past decade has been the move from tolerated informality to legal recognition. For years, nomads operated in a gray area, cycling through tourist visas while technically working illegally. Enforcement was inconsistent, and the risks felt manageable.

That era is ending. Governments have become more attentive to the presence of remote workers. Some view them as an opportunity, creating visas that acknowledge foreign income and offer legal residency. Others are tightening enforcement, restricting stays, and increasing scrutiny.

Digital nomad visas represent an attempt to bring clarity to this landscape. They formalize what was previously ambiguous, offering defined rights and obligations. Income thresholds, health insurance requirements, and background checks are common features. In exchange, nomads gain the ability to stay legally, open bank accounts, and access services without constant uncertainty.

For serious digital nomads, these pathways are transformative. They allow planning beyond a few months. They reduce stress. They make it possible to invest emotionally and financially in a place.

The trade-off is transparency. Legal residency creates tax exposure. It requires compliance. It removes the illusion of invisibility. For those willing to accept that trade, the benefits are substantial.

From Motion to Basecamp

One of the least discussed aspects of digital nomad life is how it changes over time. Constant movement, while exhilarating at first, often proves unsustainable. Packing, relocating, and re-establishing routines every few weeks erodes productivity and emotional well-being.

Many nomads respond by slowing down. They establish base cities where they spend several months at a time, traveling outward in shorter bursts. This approach preserves flexibility while restoring routine.

Basecamp living allows deeper integration: language skills improve, social networks form, healthcare becomes accessible. The city begins to feel less like a backdrop and more like a home.

This evolution is the maturation of nomadism. The goal is not endless motion, but optionality. The ability to move when desired, not because one must. Digital nomads who achieve this balance often describe a profound sense of control over their lives, one rooted not in escape but in choice.

Work, Time, and the Invisible Frictions

Living abroad while working remotely introduces subtle frictions that are easy to underestimate. Time zone differences can strain relationships with employers or clients. Meetings scheduled for convenience in the United States may fall late at night or early in the morning abroad. Over time, this misalignment can take a toll.

Some nomads adapt by choosing destinations with favorable time zones. Others negotiate asynchronous workflows. A few eventually shift their client base to align better with local hours.

These adjustments require communication and trust. Employers must be informed. Expectations must be managed. Not all organizations are willing to accommodate long-term international work, particularly when tax or data considerations arise. The digital nomad who thrives treats work arrangements as partnerships rather than entitlements. They recognize that location flexibility is a privilege that carries responsibility.

The Question of Belonging

As stays lengthen and routines settle, digital nomads confront a deeper question: where do I belong?

Temporary living can feel both liberating and isolating. Community takes time to build. Relationships deepen slowly. Without intentional effort, nomads can find themselves surrounded by people but lacking connection.

Those who succeed invest in place even while remaining mobile. They learn the language. They participate in local life. They build friendships beyond transient circles. They treat residence as more than occupancy. This investment changes the experience. The city stops being a product and starts being a relationship.

Part III: From Movement to Meaning

The hardest part of digital nomad life is rarely work, visas, or money. Those challenges are tangible: they can be researched, planned for, and solved. The deeper challenge emerges later, once the novelty wears off and the rhythm of constant motion reveals its cost.

What remains is the question of how to live not just efficiently but well. Digital nomadism promises freedom, but freedom without structure can quietly turn into drift. The difference between a fulfilling nomadic life and a draining one often lies not in where someone goes, but in how they inhabit the places they choose.

The Emotional Geography of Mobility

At first, movement feels expansive. Each new city offers stimulation, discovery, and a sense of reinvention. Old routines dissolve. Identity feels lighter. Problems seem easier at a distance.

Over time, however, the emotional weight of constant transition accumulates. Relationships remain shallow because departures are assumed. Familiarity never quite takes root. Even small tasks—finding a dentist, establishing trust with a landlord, learning local systems—must be repeated again and again.

Loneliness can appear unexpectedly, even in crowded places. It is not the absence of people that creates it, but the absence of continuity.

This is not a failure of digital nomadism. It is a natural consequence of living without anchors. Those who thrive long-term learn to create their own.

Community as Infrastructure

Just as reliable internet is essential for work, community is essential for sustainability. Digital nomads who endure are not necessarily the most adventurous, but the most intentional about relationships.

In the early stages, many rely on other nomads for connection. Co-working spaces, online forums, and social meetups provide quick entry points. These communities are valuable, but they are also transient. People arrive and leave. Bonds form quickly and dissolve just as fast.

Over time, many nomads begin to seek something more stable. They build relationships with local residents. They return to the same cafés. They volunteer, join language classes, or participate in neighborhood life. These connections take longer to form, but they last.

This shift marks a turning point. Life feels less like a series of episodes and more like a story.

Redefining Success

One of the quiet transformations digital nomads undergo is a redefinition of success. Early on, success is often measured by mobility itself: the number of countries visited, the novelty of experiences, the ability to say "yes" to movement.

Later, success looks like a routine that supports creativity rather than stifles it. It looks like work that fits into life instead of dominating it. It looks like mornings that are not rushed and evenings that are not exhausted. It looks like health, both physical and mental.

For many, this leads to fewer moves, longer stays, and the establishment of one or two anchor locations. Travel becomes intentional rather than compulsive. Motion becomes a choice rather than an obligation.

This evolution represents a refinement of freedom.

The Myth of Effortless Living

Digital nomadism is often portrayed as effortless: laptops open beside turquoise water, workdays punctuated by leisure, life optimized by geography alone. The reality is more nuanced.

Living well abroad requires discipline. Time zones must be managed. Work boundaries must be protected. Health routines must be maintained without familiar systems. Bureaucratic tasks must be handled in foreign languages and unfamiliar frameworks.

Those who succeed treat their lives as systems. They schedule rest as deliberately as work. They limit overstimulation. They choose environments that support focus rather than distraction.

This discipline is not restrictive. It is what allows freedom to last.

Identity Without a Single Place

The most profound shift digital nomads experience is in how they understand identity. Without a fixed home, traditional markers like address, neighborhood, and local status lose their centrality. Identity becomes more internal.

People begin to define themselves less by where they are and more by how they live. Values replace geography as anchors. Curiosity, adaptability, and self-reliance become core traits.

This can be deeply empowering. It can also be disorienting. Without a clear sense of belonging to a place, some struggle to answer simple questions. "Where are you from?" "Where do you live?" "Where is home?"

Over time, many discover that home does not have to be singular. It can be layered. One place for work, another for rest, a third for family. Or it can be portable, rooted in routines and relationships rather than coordinates.

The goal is not to avoid attachment, but to choose it consciously.

When Nomadism Ends—and What Comes After

For many, digital nomadism is a chapter rather than a permanent state. Careers evolve. Relationships deepen. Children arrive. Health priorities change. The desire for stability grows.

This does not negate the value of the nomadic years. On the contrary, those years often reshape priorities permanently. People who have lived and worked abroad rarely return unchanged. They carry with them a broader perspective, a recalibrated sense of need, and a deeper appreciation for systems that work.

Some transition into traditional expatriation, settling long-term in a chosen country. Others return to the United States with clearer boundaries and different expectations. A few continue to live between worlds, maintaining mobility while embracing selective rootedness.

Digital nomadism, at its best, is not an escape from responsibility, but an education in choice.

Living Deliberately in a World of Options

The deeper promise of digital nomadism is not freedom from place, but freedom with place, the ability to choose environments that support who you are becoming, rather than remaining where you happen to be.

This ability carries responsibility. It requires awareness of privilege, respect for local communities, and an understanding that mobility is not neutral. How nomads live affects housing markets, culture, and social dynamics. Living abroad ethically means participating thoughtfully rather than consuming casually.

Those who embrace this responsibility find that digital nomadism becomes more than a lifestyle. It becomes a practice—of attentiveness, adaptability, and intentional living.

The Arc Completed

When we began, we explored how climate change reshapes physical viability, how the global economy redistributes opportunity, and how politics determines stability and rights. Digital nomadism is one way individuals respond to these forces in real time.

It is not the only response, nor is it a universal solution. But for those whose work allows it, it offers a rare combination of agency and perspective. It allows people to live experimentally, to test different ways of being, and to design lives that are responsive rather than reactive.The digital nomad is not someone without roots. They are someone learning where to place their roots.

Now, let's turn from philosophy to execution, exploring the practical logistics of moving abroad—packing, shipping, storage, banking, and the small but consequential decisions that determine whether the transition feels chaotic or controlled.

Because a life in motion still needs a foundation, and building that foundation well is what turns movement into freedom.

Chapter 6

RETIREMENT ABROAD

A NEW CHAPTER IN A NEW CLIMATE

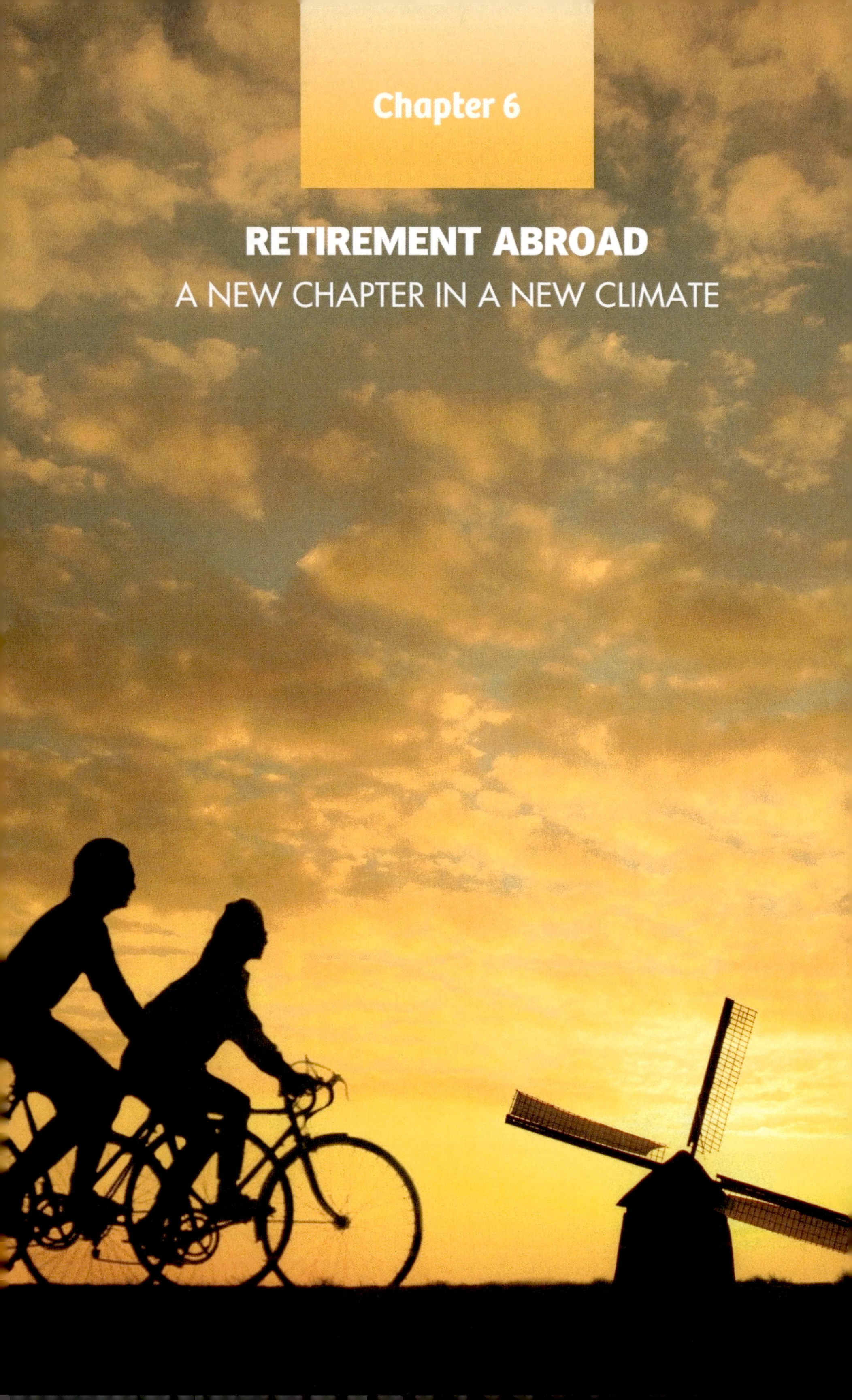

Part I: Leaving the Old Dream

For much of the twentieth century, the American idea of retirement followed a familiar script. After decades of work, a person was meant to slow down, settle in place, and enjoy the rewards of stability. Retirement was not a beginning so much as a gentle deceleration—fewer obligations, fewer risks, fewer surprises. A paid-off home, proximity to family, warm weather, and modest recreation formed the ideal. Florida, Arizona, Southern California, and a scattering of resort towns absorbed millions of retirees who expected continuity more than transformation.

That vision was shaped by a specific historical moment. Housing was affordable, pensions were common, healthcare costs were manageable, and the dollar traveled far even within national borders. Retirement was conceived as a domestic phase of life, anchored to the same systems—financial, political, cultural—that had governed adulthood. Leaving the country entirely, especially in later life, was considered eccentric or impractical, something undertaken by diplomats, adventurers, or those with complicated pasts rather than ordinary Americans.

William's life followed that traditional arc—until it didn't. A theoretical physicist by training, he built a long, successful career in aerospace and computer consulting, living and working across California, Alaska, and Texas. He was intellectually restless but institutionally conventional, firmly embedded in American professional life. Yet in his mid-sixties, as his career began to wind down, he started spending extended periods visiting a childhood friend in Veracruz, Mexico. What began as regular visits slowly became a rhythm of life.

Over time, William decided to buy a condominium in Veracruz. Under ordinary circumstances, an American citizen cannot own property near the Mexican coast. But William approached the problem methodically. He formed a company, continued doing limited consulting work, and had the company purchase the property. It was not fast, and it was not simple, but it was legal, deliberate, and durable. He lived in Mexico for nearly three decades, building a life that balanced familiarity with reinvention. When his health finally failed, he returned to the United States to be near his son—this was not until he was ninety-five years old. By any reasonable measure, his retirement abroad was a success.

William's story does not resemble retreat, nor does it fit the caricature of escape. It reflects something else entirely: the quiet emergence of retirement as a phase of agency rather than withdrawal.

Retirement as an extension of curiosity and agency

Today, a growing number of Americans approaching or entering retirement are following a path like William's, looking outward instead of inward, across national borders rather than state lines. They are not merely downsizing or relocating to cheaper ZIP codes; they are resettling their lives in unfamiliar cultures, languages, and legal systems. Some do so seasonally, while others make permanent moves, selling homes they once assumed they would die in. Still others leave even before visiting their new country, trusting research, online communities, and intuition more than nostalgia. This shift is not driven by a single factor. It is the product of converging pressures that have quietly reshaped what retirement means in America.

Economics is the most obvious factor: housing costs have outpaced incomes for decades, healthcare expenses have become unpredictable and often catastrophic, and inflation has eroded the purchasing power of savings that were once thought sufficient. Even retirees who planned carefully find themselves wondering how long their money will last and what tradeoffs will be required to make it last longer.

But economics alone does not explain the scale or intensity of the movement. Many retirees who choose to live abroad could afford to remain in the United States if they wished. What they are responding to is not just cost, but climate in the broadest sense—social, political, environmental, and psychological. The United States has become louder, faster, more polarized, and more anxious, particularly for those who remember a different rhythm of life. For retirees, who no longer benefit from the dynamism and opportunity of a high-stress economy, the downsides of that environment are increasingly difficult to ignore.

There is also the matter of safety and predictability. Gun violence, political volatility, strained institutions, and the constant churn of crisis-driven media have altered the emotional landscape of daily life. Retirement was once imagined as a time of peace and reflection. For many Americans, that promise feels harder to fulfill at home than it once did. Living abroad is not an escape from reality, but it can feel like a recalibration—an opportunity to step outside a system that no longer feels aligned with one's values or temperament.

Environmental pressures compound these concerns. Climate change is no longer an abstract future problem but a lived experience, particularly for older Americans. Heat waves, wildfires, hurricanes, floods, and droughts increasingly shape where and how people can live. Insurance markets have begun to fracture under this strain, making entire regions difficult or impossible to insure affordably. For retirees on fixed incomes, these risks are not theoretical. They are line items, renewal notices, evacuation plans, and sleepless nights. Moving abroad can be a way to seek not only beauty and affordability, but resilience—places where infrastructure, geography, and governance offer a measure of stability in an uncertain era.

At the same time, the world has become more accessible to retirees than ever before. Air travel is cheaper and more reliable than in past generations. English is widely spoken in many countries, and translation technology has reduced language barriers. Online banking, telemedicine, and international shipping allow people to maintain financial and social ties across continents. What once required a complete severing of connections can now be managed with a smartphone and a stable internet connection.

Equally important is the changing psychology of aging itself. Today's retirees are healthier, more educated, and more globally aware than previous generations. Many traveled extensively during their working years, whether for business or pleasure. They are comfortable navigating unfamiliar environments and less willing to accept the idea that later life should be geographically and intellectually narrow. Retirement abroad is not seen as abandonment of home, but as an extension of curiosity and agency.

For some, the decision is pragmatic. Living abroad allows Social Security income, pensions, or investment distributions to stretch further, transforming a constrained retirement into a comfortable one. For others, the motivation is emotional or philosophical. Retirement becomes a chance to live deliberately, to choose surroundings that support daily pleasures rather than constant consumption, to prioritize walkability, community, food, and time over accumulation and speed.

Whatever the forces driving the decision, what unites these retirees is not dissatisfaction alone, but a reimagining of what is possible. They are not fleeing the United States so much as questioning the assumption that it must remain the default setting for the rest of their lives. Retirement abroad offers an alternative—one in which aging is not synonymous with contraction, and where place is an active choice rather than a passive inheritance.

This choice is not made lightly. Leaving one's home country later in life carries emotional weight. Family ties, lifelong friendships, cultural familiarity, and a sense of belonging are powerful anchors. Many wrestle with guilt about distance from children and grandchildren, or fear that they will become strangers to the places and people that shaped them. Others worry about vulnerability: what happens when health declines, when bureaucracy becomes confusing, or when language barriers feel heavier with age. Yet staying put carries its own risks. Loneliness, financial anxiety, environmental exposure, and a sense of stagnation can be just as destabilizing as uncertainty.

Retirement abroad is often less about chasing novelty than about choosing the conditions under which one wants to age, reflecting a broader shift in how Americans relate to place. Just as digital nomads redefined work as something that could be detached from geography, retirees are redefining later life as something that can be re-located, restructured, and reimagined. Retiring abroad opens the door to a different kind of stability, one rooted not in familiarity alone, but in alignment across values, resources, and environment.

The decision is deeply personal, shaped by finances, health, temperament, and family dynamics. But it is also undeniably collective, emerging from shared pressures and shared realizations about what the future may hold. It is an acknowledgment that the world has changed, and that aging within it requires flexibility, courage, and intentionality.

Now, let's shift from motivation to mechanics, to explore how retirees navigate the practical realities of living abroad: residency rules, healthcare systems, financial planning, and the often-overlooked challenges that determine whether the dream becomes sustainable—or dissolves under its own complexity.

Part II: Making It Work

The romance of retiring abroad often begins with imagery: a café table in a sunlit plaza, a morning walk along the sea, a slower rhythm shaped by conversation rather than schedules. Yet the success of such a life depends less on aesthetics and more on structure. Once the decision to explore retirement abroad moves from aspiration to intention, retirees confront a dense web of practical considerations that determine whether life overseas will feel liberating or precarious. This is where fantasy yields to logistics, and where many early dreams are either refined into sustainable plans or quietly abandoned.

The first and most immediate reality is legal presence. Unlike short-term travel, retirement abroad requires permission to stay. Every country regulates who may reside within its borders, for how long, and under what conditions. Retirees quickly learn that visas and residence permits are not interchangeable, and that overstaying a tourist allowance can derail long-term plans. Many countries offer retirement-specific residence programs with requirements such as proof of steady income, savings, or pensions designed to ensure that retirees will not become dependent on local social services and can support themselves without competing for local employment.

The paperwork can feel daunting, particularly for Americans accustomed to informal domestic mobility. Documents must often be apostilled, translated, and submitted in rigid formats. Processing times may be slow, opaque, or unpredictable. Regulations can change midstream, leaving applicants scrambling to adapt. Yet for those who persist, residency brings stability: the right to lease property long-term, register locally, access healthcare systems, and live without the constant pressure of visa expiration. Over time, the bureaucracy becomes less intimidating, and many retirees report that navigating foreign systems sharpens a sense of agency they feared losing with age.

Healthcare is often the most emotionally charged concern. For Americans, the idea of leaving Medicare triggers understandable anxiety. Medicare does not generally cover care outside the United States, and many retirees assume this makes overseas living impractical or risky. In practice, the opposite is often true. Many countries provide high-quality healthcare at costs that are dramatically lower than those in the U.S., both for routine care and for major procedures. Retirees may purchase private insurance, enroll in national health systems where permitted, or pay out of pocket for services that would be financially ruinous back home.

The adjustment is not merely financial but psychological. Healthcare abroad is often less transactional and less hurried, with longer consultations and fewer layers of billing complexity. However, it may also involve different standards, protocols, and expectations. Preventive care may be emphasized differently. Prescription practices may vary. Some retirees feel reassured by the simplicity and affordability; others miss the familiarity of U.S. specialists and technology. Many choose hybrid strategies, maintaining a relationship with doctors in the United States while relying on local care for everyday needs.

Financial planning underpins every aspect of retirement abroad. Fixed incomes behave differently across borders. Currency exchange rates introduce both opportunity and risk, turning retirement budgets into moving targets. A strong dollar can dramatically enhance purchasing power, while a weakening one can compress margins overnight. Savvy retirees learn to diversify accounts, maintain access to U.S. banking systems, and manage cash flow carefully. They may strategically time large purchases or transfers, and they often develop a more nuanced understanding of money than they ever needed during their working years.

Taxes present another layer of complexity. U.S. citizens remain subject to U.S. taxation regardless of residence, an obligation that surprises many first-time expatriates. Filing requirements persist, even when income is modest or primarily foreign-sourced. Some retirees benefit from tax treaties that reduce double taxation, while others must plan carefully to avoid unintended consequences. Retirement income streams such as Social Security, pensions, and investment distributions are treated differently depending on the country and tax structure. The administrative burden can feel heavy, but for those who plan well, the overall financial picture often remains favorable compared to remaining in the United States.

Housing decisions shape daily life more profoundly than any spreadsheet. Retirees must decide whether to rent or buy, whether to live in urban centers or rural areas, and how closely they wish to integrate into local communities. Renting offers flexibility and lower commitment, particularly during the exploratory phase. Buying can provide long-term stability but may introduce legal and inheritance complications. Property markets abroad often operate differently, with fewer disclosures, different financing norms, and stronger tenant protections.

The Emotional Journey Abroad

Beyond legality and cost lies the subtler question of belonging. Language barriers, even when manageable, can create distance. Daily tasks that once felt effortless—visiting a doctor, dealing with utilities, resolving a dispute—require patience and humility. Some retirees embrace this learning curve, finding satisfaction in mastering new systems and forging relationships across cultural divides. Others struggle with isolation, particularly if they settle in areas with limited expatriate communities or make insufficient effort to integrate.

Social life abroad does not automatically materialize: it must be built deliberately. Retirees who thrive tend to cultivate routines that anchor them: language classes, volunteer work, regular cafés, walking routes, clubs, or religious communities. They learn that integration is less about fluency than consistency—showing up, being curious, and accepting moments of awkwardness as part of the process. Over time, what felt foreign becomes familiar, and what felt isolating becomes communal.

Distance from family remains the most persistent emotional challenge. Technology allows for constant communication, but cannot replace physical presence. Milestones may be missed, grandchildren grow quickly, and emergencies can create logistical strain. Many retirees navigate this by structuring their lives flexibly, maintaining the ability to return to the United States for extended visits or to respond quickly when needed. Some choose locations with excellent air connectivity; others structure their year around seasons and family calendars. Retirement abroad often becomes a rhythm rather than a relocation.

What emerges from these practical realities is a clearer understanding of what retirement abroad truly requires: adaptability, patience, and a willingness to live with ambiguity. It rewards curiosity, resilience, and thoughtful planning. Those who succeed do not eliminate risk; they manage it differently. They trade one set of uncertainties for another, often finding that the new ones feel more tolerable, more human-scaled, and more aligned with how they wish to spend their remaining years.

Part III: Redefining Home, Aging, and Belonging

For many retirees, the most profound consequences of moving abroad are not financial or logistical but existential. What begins as a practical decision—a desire for lower costs, better weather, more manageable healthcare—alters the way people understand aging, identity, and the meaning of home itself, and prompts an examination of how they understand themselves within the arc of their lives. In leaving the familiar behind, retirees are forced to confront assumptions they may not have examined in decades: what it means to belong somewhere, what constitutes security, and how much of identity is shaped by place.

In the United States, aging is frequently framed as a problem to be managed. Retirement communities are often segregated by age, suburbanized, and insulated from the rhythms of daily economic life. Older adults are encouraged to remain independent, but independence is narrowly defined as the absence of need rather than the presence of connection. As physical capacity declines, social worlds often shrink. The result is a paradox in which retirees may possess comfort and convenience yet feel increasingly invisible.

Living abroad disrupts this pattern. In many countries, older adults remain embedded in public life. Cities and towns are designed for walking rather than driving, encouraging daily movement and chance encounters. Cafés, markets, and plazas cultivate social infrastructure, providing informal spaces where people of all ages mix. Aging becomes more visible, but also more normalized. Retirees are not hidden away; they are participants in the everyday life of their communities.

This shift can be disorienting at first. Without the cultural cues that once reinforced identity—career titles, long-standing social roles, familiar status markers—retirees abroad often experience a temporary erosion of self-definition. They are no longer known quantities. They must introduce themselves anew, sometimes repeatedly, and often in a language that does not fully capture nuance or humor. Yet this vulnerability can be strangely liberating. Freed from the expectations of who they were, retirees gain space to explore who they are becoming.

Many report a renewed sense of presence. Without the constant pull of productivity and consumption that characterizes much of American life, days slow down. Time is structured less by obligation and more by ritual: morning walks, shared meals, and conversations that are not rushed. This rhythm supports reflection and attentiveness, qualities often squeezed out during working years. Life becomes less about filling time and more about inhabiting it.

The concept of home undergoes a parallel transformation. For Americans, home is often associated with ownership, permanence, and accumulation. A house represents stability and identity, a physical manifestation of success and belonging. When retirees move abroad, particularly as renters, this equation shifts. Home becomes less about possession and more about practice. It is found in routines rather than walls, in relationships rather than deeds.

This does not mean that attachment disappears. Many retirees maintain deep emotional ties to the United States, returning regularly to visit family and reconnect with familiar landscapes. Home becomes plural rather than singular, existing in multiple places at once, each serving different emotional needs. One place may offer roots and memory, another lightness and possibility. The ability to hold these truths simultaneously reflects a more flexible understanding of belonging.

Aging abroad also reframes the relationship between dependence and dignity. In the United States, reliance on others is often stigmatized, particularly for older adults. Abroad, interdependence is more openly acknowledged. Asking for help is not always a failure; it is part of social exchange. Retirees who struggle initially with language or bureaucracy often find that receiving assistance creates connection rather than embarrassment. Over time, these interactions foster mutual recognition and trust.

There are, of course, moments of doubt. Illness, bereavement, or sudden change can sharpen the awareness of distance from family and familiar systems. Some retirees eventually return to the United States, concluding that the emotional costs outweigh the benefits. Others adapt by modifying their arrangements, spending more time stateside, or relocating closer to international hubs. Retirement abroad is not a one-way door; it is a continuum of choices that can be revised as circumstances evolve.

What distinguishes those who thrive is not the absence of difficulty but the presence of intentionality. Retirees who approach life abroad as a static solution often become disillusioned when novelty fades.

Chapter 7

EMIGRATION

MAKING THE MOVE

Part I: From Dream to Decision

For many Americans, the idea of moving abroad begins as an imagined life—a projection rather than a plan. It surfaces during vacations or late-night searches, fueled by images of sunlit piazzas, coastal villages, or mountain towns where life appears simpler and more humane. In these early stages, emigration feels aspirational, even romantic. It is less about departure than about possibility, less about leaving than about arriving somewhere better.

If the idea has staying power, it eventually changes character. The fantasy confronts friction. Questions intrude: How would this actually work? What would it mean to live somewhere rather than merely visit? How would money move, healthcare function, taxes be paid, and legal status be maintained? The notion of travel gives way to the far more consequential idea of emigration.

Marie reached this inflection point through ancestry rather than imagination. One of her parents was born in Italy, giving her a legitimate claim to Italian citizenship by descent. On paper, the path appeared straightforward. In practice, it was anything but. Months of effort unfolded across two bureaucracies—the Italian consulate in San Francisco and local authorities in Italy—each with its own procedures, interpretations, and delays. Just as resolution seemed near, her application stalled over a technicality: a document that had not been notarized in precisely the required manner. The mistake did not invalidate her claim, but it did suspend it indefinitely. Her experience underscores a lesson common to emigration: even when eligibility is real, progress is rarely linear, and success is seldom guaranteed.

Emigration is not simply extended travel. It is a structural shift in one's life, a reorientation that touches nearly every system that once operated invisibly in the background. In the United States, residency, banking, taxation, and healthcare are largely frictionless by virtue of familiarity. Abroad, these systems become explicit. They demand attention, documentation, and compliance. The transition is not just geographic; it is administrative, legal, and psychological.

Many Americans underestimate this distinction because the modern world makes movement appear deceptively easy. Flights are cheap, borders are porous to tourists, and digital infrastructure allows people to work, bank, and communicate across continents. This creates the illusion that living abroad is simply traveling longer. In reality, the moment one crosses the threshold from visitor to resident—whether formally or informally—the relationship with the host country changes. Rights expand, but so do obligations.

Living abroad, even part-time, places an individual inside a legal framework not designed for casual participation. Visa rules define how long one may stay and under what conditions. Residency permits establish obligations related to registration, taxation, and healthcare. These rules are not arbitrary, nor are they optional. They are expressions of sovereignty, and they shape the daily realities of expatriate life more than scenery or culture ever could.

This is why emigration often unfolds in stages. Few people make a clean break on the first attempt. Instead, many begin with extended stays, testing places over seasons, learning how it feels to live rather than visit. They rent apartments instead of hotels, shop at local markets instead of in tourist districts, and attempt mundane tasks like opening bank accounts or seeing doctors. These experiences strip away illusion quickly; they also clarify intention.

At some point, a decision emerges. The individual realizes that what they are doing is no longer travel. They are building routines, forming relationships, and organizing their life around a place that is not their country of origin. This is the moment when emigration becomes real—not because a visa has been granted, but because their center of gravity has shifted.

This shift brings with it a new awareness of time. Tourists live on borrowed time, conscious of departure dates and return flights. Emigrants, by contrast, must think in terms of continuity. How long can I stay? What happens next year? What happens if rules change? Time becomes cyclical rather than linear, structured around renewals, registrations, and compliance. This can feel constraining at first, but it also introduces a form of stability absent from perpetual motion.

For Americans, this adjustment is particularly stark. The United States is geographically vast and internally diverse, allowing people to experience change without crossing national borders. Moving from New York to Arizona or California to Texas can feel like entering a different country without the legal complications of emigration. As a result, many Americans reach midlife or retirement with little experience navigating foreign bureaucracies or residency regimes. When they attempt to do so later in life, the learning curve can feel steep.

This unfamiliarity is not a disadvantage so much as a rite of passage. Emigration forces individuals to become literate in systems they once took for granted. It requires attentiveness to law, process, and cultural norms. In doing so, it often cultivates a renewed sense of agency. Those who succeed are not necessarily the most adventurous or wealthy, but the most patient and prepared.

One of the earliest lessons emigrants learn is that intent matters. Countries distinguish sharply between visitors and residents, even when outward behavior appears similar. A person who spends three months each year in the same place as a tourist is treated differently from someone who rents long-term housing, registers locally, or seeks access to services. These distinctions are not merely semantic. They determine tax exposure, healthcare eligibility, and legal protections.

This is why the language of emigration is important. To "emigrate" is to acknowledge that one is entering into a relationship with another country. It implies respect for local rules and an understanding that privileges are conditional. It also implies a degree of humility. Unlike travel, which centers the visitor's experience, emigration centers adaptation. The emigrant must learn how things are done, not how they wish they were done.

For some, this realization is sobering enough to halt the process entirely. They discover that what they want is not emigration but escape—a temporary reprieve rather than a new foundation. Seasonal living, extended travel, and partial relocation can all be valid choices. But clarity matters. Problems arise when individuals attempt to live as residents while behaving as tourists, relying on loopholes and informal arrangements that eventually collapse.

This tension is most visible in regions with high American interest and strict residency frameworks, particularly Europe. The freedom to move within much of the continent as a visitor can mask the reality that long-term residency is tightly regulated. Many Americans are surprised to learn that enjoying a place for three months does not confer any special claim to remain longer. Borders that feel open are, in fact, governed by precise calendars and enforcement mechanisms.

The popular imagination often lags behind this reality. Online forums and anecdotal advice can create the impression that rules are flexible or inconsistently applied. While enforcement may vary, the underlying legal structures do not. Those who ignore them do so at increasing risk, especially as immigration systems become more digitized and coordinated. What once slipped through cracks is now more likely to be recorded, flagged, and penalized.

The decision to emigrate, then, is ultimately a decision to engage with reality on new terms. It requires abandoning the comfort of invisibility and accepting that one's presence must be justified, documented, and renewed. For many Americans, this is the most difficult psychological shift. The freedom to simply be somewhere—to exist without explanation—is something they have rarely questioned. Abroad, that freedom is conditional.

Yet for those willing to make this adjustment, emigration offers something profound in return. It provides access not just to new places, but to new ways of structuring life. It invites individuals to reconsider assumptions about work, aging, consumption, and community. It challenges them to build coherence across borders rather than within them.

Part II: Pathways, Permissions, and the Limits of Flexibility

Once the decision to emigrate becomes concrete, the question shifts from whether it is desirable to whether it is legally and practically possible. This is the stage at which many Americans encounter their first real constraints. Desire, income, and enthusiasm are not sufficient on their own. Emigration is mediated through formal pathways, each defined by a host country's priorities, anxieties, and administrative capacity. Understanding these pathways is essential, not only to gaining entry, but to building a life that is durable rather than provisional.

At the most basic level, countries distinguish between presence and residence. Presence is temporary and conditional, governed by short-term permissions granted to visitors. Residence implies continuity and intent, signaling that a person wishes to anchor their life, even partially, within a country's borders. This distinction is reflected in visa categories, registration requirements, and enforcement mechanisms. The transition from presence to residence is the legal heart of emigration.

Many Americans begin their overseas lives under the umbrella of tourist status. This is natural and often prudent. Tourist stays allow individuals to test locations, seasons, and daily routines without committing to a legal framework that may later prove ill-suited. Yet tourist status is, by design, restrictive: it prohibits work, limits duration, and offers no pathway to permanence. It is a viewing platform, not a foundation.

The constraints of tourist status become most visible in regions that coordinate border policy across multiple countries. In much of Europe, Americans are permitted to remain for a defined number of days within a rolling period, regardless of how many countries they visit. This system creates a sense of openness while quietly enforcing strict temporal boundaries. For casual travelers, these limits are invisible. For aspiring emigrants, they become the ticking clock around which life must be organized. The modern system governing short-term travel across much of Europe traces its origins to the Schengen Agreement, signed in 1985 in the village of Schengen. This agreement laid the foundation for what is now known as the Schengen Area—a group of European countries that have abolished internal border controls, allowing passport-free movement between them.

Under today's Schengen rules, citizens of countries such as the United States (who do not require a visa for short stays) may enter the Schengen Area for tourism, business meetings, or similar non-remunerated activities. The key limitation is the "90/180 rule": a non-EU visitor can stay for up to 90 days within any rolling 180-day period across all Schengen countries combined, not per country.

Importantly, the Schengen Area is distinct from the European Union. While many Schengen countries are EU members, not all EU countries are in Schengen, and a few non-EU countries participate in Schengen. What unifies the system is not EU membership itself, but participation in the shared border and visa framework established by the Schengen Agreement and its later implementing conventions.

For travelers, this means that once you enter one Schengen country, you can generally move freely among others without additional border checks—but your total time across the entire area is counted toward that 90-day limit.

To navigate this, many Americans experiment with what has come to be known as the "Schengen-shuffle"—moving between jurisdictions to reset their allowable stay. By alternating time between coordinated zones and neighboring countries with independent rules, they extend their time abroad without formal residency. When executed carefully, this approach can be lawful and can support a nomadic or seasonal lifestyle for years. But it is inherently unstable. It requires constant vigilance, careful tracking of days, and a willingness to remain in motion.

More importantly, the Schengen-shuffle does not confer the rights or protections of residence. Those who rely on it remain outsiders in legal terms, unable to register locally, access public services, or establish formal ties. Banking, leasing property, and obtaining healthcare become more complicated. Over time, the psychological cost of impermanence often outweighs the convenience of flexibility. For those seeking continuity, the shuffle is a bridge, not a destination.

Temporary residency programs represent the next level of commitment. These permits allow individuals to live in a country for extended periods, and are often renewable annually or biannually. They are the backbone of modern emigration, designed to attract retirees, remote workers, investors, and others who can support themselves without displacing local labor. Requirements vary widely but typically include proof of income or savings and health insurance, housing arrangements, and background checks.

For Americans, temporary residency often feels like a reasonable compromise. It offers stability without irrevocability, allowing individuals to build a life while retaining the option to leave. Yet temporary status comes with its own form of uncertainty: renewals are not guaranteed, rules may change, income thresholds may rise. What begins as a straightforward process can become more demanding over time, particularly as governments adjust policies in response to housing pressure, political sentiment, or administrative overload.

Permanent residency represents a deeper form of commitment. It signals that the host country recognizes the individual as a long-term member of society, entitled to remain indefinitely under defined conditions. Permanent status often follows years of temporary residence and requires evidence of integration, compliance, and continuity. For many Americans, permanent residency is an aspirational milestone rather than an immediate goal. It offers security without requiring renunciation of original citizenship.

Citizenship occupies a different category entirely. It is not merely permission to stay, but membership in a political community. Naturalization typically demands long residence, language proficiency, and cultural integration. Some countries offer accelerated paths through ancestry or marriage, but these are exceptions rather than norms. For most American emigrants, citizenship is not necessary to achieve their objectives and may introduce complexities related to allegiance, taxation, or identity that outweigh its benefits.

What unites all these pathways is the principle of conditionality. No country grants residence lightly. Each imposes criteria designed to align immigration with national interest. These criteria are not moral judgments; they are administrative filters that prioritize economic self-sufficiency, social stability, and regulatory compliance. Emigrants who understand this framework are less likely to feel frustrated or singled out. Those who resist it often experience the process as arbitrary or hostile.

A common source of tension arises when Americans attempt to live abroad informally while expecting formal benefits. This might include working remotely on a tourist status, accessing healthcare without proper enrollment, or assuming that long-term presence will be tolerated without documentation. Such arrangements may persist for a time, particularly in countries with limited enforcement capacity, but they remain vulnerable. Changes in leadership, technology, or policy can expose informal residents overnight, turning years of quiet living into urgent legal problems.

The global trend is toward greater coordination and digitization of immigration systems. Entry and exit records are increasingly automated. Data is shared across borders. What once relied on stamps and discretion now rests on databases and algorithms. For emigrants, this means that compliance is no longer optional or obscure. It is traceable, cumulative, and consequential.

At the same time, flexibility has not disappeared. Many countries actively court foreign residents who bring income, skills, or demographic balance. New visa categories emerge regularly, reflecting shifts in economic strategy and social need. Digital nomad programs, retirement visas, and investment-based residencies are all products of this evolution. Emigration today is not a single path but a landscape of options that reward attentiveness and adaptability.

For Americans navigating this landscape, the challenge is not simply to find a visa, but to choose a structure that aligns with how they actually live. A person who wants deep community integration may find perpetual temporariness exhausting. Someone who values mobility may chafe under the obligations of permanent status. Emigration is not a one-size-fits-all solution; it is a design problem, requiring clarity about priorities and tolerance for tradeoffs.

This is where many emigrants pause, reassess, and recalibrate. The process of seeking permission forces reflection. It asks not only where one wants to live, but how. How much stability is necessary? How much bureaucracy is acceptable? How much uncertainty is tolerable? These questions do not have universal answers. They are negotiated individually, shaped by temperament as much as circumstance.

Part III: Building a Life Beyond Borders

Securing the right to stay is only the first step in emigration. Living abroad requires rebuilding the invisible scaffolding of daily life—banking, healthcare, taxation, and social belonging. Once the paperwork is approved and the novelty of arrival fades, emigrants confront the quieter, more demanding task of building a functioning life within unfamiliar systems. This is where emigration succeeds or fails—not at the border, but in the daily negotiations that turn permission into belonging.

The most immediate of these systems is banking. Money, which moves invisibly through familiar institutions, becomes a source of friction abroad. Opening accounts may require residency cards, tax numbers, proof of address, and, in some cases, personal introductions. Anti-money laundering rules, designed to combat global financial crime, have made banks cautious, particularly with American clients subject to extraterritorial reporting regimes. Many emigrants learn to maintain parallel financial lives, keeping U.S. accounts active while establishing local ones for everyday expenses.

This dual structure requires vigilance. Transfers must be timed and tracked. Exchange rates fluctuate. Fees accumulate. Yet over time, emigrants develop fluency in which institutions are flexible, which processes can be automated, and which require in-person persistence. Financial independence abroad depends less on wealth than on organization. Those who master these systems gain confidence; those who do not often feel perpetually unsettled.

Healthcare integration follows a similar arc. Beyond insurance policies and eligibility rules lies the practical matter of accessing care. Finding doctors, understanding referral systems, and navigating pharmacies can feel disorienting at first. Medical records may not transfer seamlessly. Terminology may differ. Yet many emigrants find that once established, healthcare abroad is more relational and less adversarial than in the United States. Costs are transparent. Visits are unrushed. Preventive care is often emphasized over intervention.

Still, health remains a central anxiety, particularly as people age. Serious illness or declining mobility can prompt reassessment of location and support networks. Some emigrants plan explicitly for this contingency, choosing countries with robust healthcare infrastructure or proximity to family. Others accept uncertainty as the price of autonomy. Emigration does not eliminate vulnerability; it reframes it.

Taxation is another domain where assumptions quickly erode. Americans often discover that emigration complicates rather than simplifies their fiscal lives. Filing obligations persist. Reporting requirements expand. Foreign accounts trigger disclosure thresholds. Tax treaties mitigate some double taxation, but they also introduce complexity. Many emigrants eventually seek professional guidance, recognizing that compliance is not merely a legal obligation but a form of risk management.

Housing, too, reveals the gap between expectation and reality. Leases may be shorter or longer than anticipated. Tenant protections may be stronger or weaker. Maintenance responsibilities may fall differently. Cultural norms around privacy, noise, and communal space can surprise even experienced travelers. Over time, emigrants adjust, learning which compromises are tolerable and which are not. Home becomes less about control and more about fit.

The most subtle challenge is social integration. Emigration disrupts social capital accumulated over a lifetime. Familiar roles disappear. Casual interactions must be rebuilt from scratch. Language barriers, even when modest, slow connection. Some retreat into expatriate enclaves, finding comfort in shared language and experience. Others push deliberately into local networks, accepting discomfort as the cost of belonging. Most navigate a middle path, balancing familiarity with exposure.

What emerges from these efforts is a recalibrated sense of self. Successful emigrants become more attentive, more patient, and often more resilient. They learn to read systems rather than assume them. They become adept at asking for help, at observing before acting, at adapting expectations to context. This is not a loss of identity but an expansion of it. Life abroad sharpens awareness of what is cultural, what is personal, and what is negotiable.

At the same time, emigration forces confrontation with impermanence. Rules change. Political winds shift. Visas expire. Relationships evolve. The stability once associated with home becomes conditional. For some, this is unsettling. For others, it is clarifying. Emigration teaches that security is not guaranteed by geography but constructed through flexibility, planning, and community.

Importantly, emigration does not require total rupture. Many Americans who live abroad maintain strong ties to home.

Becoming the Author of Your Life Abroad

What ultimately distinguishes emigration from other forms of mobility is that it forces a reckoning with authorship. In the United States, much of life unfolds along prewritten tracks. Education, work, housing, healthcare, and retirement are structured by institutions that operate with minimal individual negotiation. Even dissatisfaction is often experienced passively, as something endured rather than redesigned. Emigration disrupts this default, placing responsibility squarely back in the hands of the individual.

This responsibility can feel heavy. There is no central authority ensuring that systems align neatly or that mistakes are easily reversed. Misjudging a visa category, misunderstanding a tax obligation, or choosing the wrong location can have real consequences. Yet this same exposure sharpens decision-making. Emigrants become planners not because they enjoy complexity, but because complexity demands it. Over time, many report a sense of security emerging from this vigilance. Knowing that stability is constructed rather than assumed produces a more realistic, less fragile confidence.

Emigration also reshapes the experience of risk. In the United States, risk is often hidden within large systems—healthcare plans, insurance markets, employer benefits—that promise protection while frequently delivering uncertainty. Abroad, risk is more visible but often more bounded. Healthcare costs are known in advance. Housing markets are less financialized. Daily expenses are predictable.

While institutional backstops may be thinner, the range of possible outcomes is often narrower. For some, this tradeoff feels profoundly stabilizing.

Over time, the distinction between "here" and "there" softens. The host country ceases to be exotic, while the country of origin becomes less central to daily life. News from home feels

louder, faster, and more abstract. Local concerns—municipal decisions, neighborhood rhythms, seasonal changes—take precedence. This is not a rejection of one identity in favor of another, but a redistribution of attention. Emigration teaches that identity is not rooted exclusively in birthplace, but also in participation.

Yet emigration is not universally liberating. For some, the accumulation of friction outweighs the benefits. Loneliness persists. Language remains a barrier. Bureaucracy becomes exhausting rather than manageable. In such cases, returning is not failure but data. Emigration is an experiment, and not all experiments confirm their hypotheses. What matters is that the choice to return is informed rather than reactive, grounded in experience rather than fear.

This reversibility is one of the least acknowledged strengths of modern emigration. Unlike previous generations, today's emigrants are rarely cut off from their countries of origin. Flights are frequent. Communication is constant. Legal status can be relinquished or reestablished. The move abroad does not have to be permanent to be meaningful. Even temporary emigration can permanently alter perspective, recalibrating expectations about cost, pace, and possibility.

At a societal level, the growing number of Americans living abroad reflects a quiet renegotiation of the relationship between citizen and state. Loyalty is no longer expressed solely through physical presence. Participation becomes selective rather than total. Individuals choose which systems they engage deeply and which they observe from a distance. This trend challenges traditional notions of national belonging but also reflects a world in which borders remain powerful while lives become increasingly transnational.

Emigration, then, is neither escape nor abandonment. It is a form of adaptation. In an era defined by economic volatility, political polarization, and environmental stress, the ability to relocate—legally, deliberately, and thoughtfully—has become a form of resilience. Those who emigrate are not necessarily rejecting their home country; they are responding to changing conditions with mobility rather than immobility.

For Americans contemplating this move, the most important question is not where to go, but why. Emigration magnifies intention. It rewards clarity and punishes ambiguity. Those who approach it as a solution to all dissatisfaction are likely to be disappointed. Those who see it as a way to align daily life with deeply held values are more likely to find coherence.

In the end, making the move abroad is less about crossing borders than crossing thresholds—between assumption and intention, familiarity and choice. Emigration requires patience, humility, and tolerance for uncertainty. It also offers perspective, autonomy, and the rare opportunity to design life rather than inherit it.

For those willing to do the work, emigration becomes a way of living that accepts complexity in exchange for agency, and uncertainty in exchange for authorship over one's own life.

Chapter 8

MEDICINE WITHOUT BORDERS

HEALTHCARE ABROAD FOR AMERICAN EXPATS

Part I: Unlearning the American System

For Americans who have spent a lifetime navigating the U.S. healthcare system, the idea of living abroad often triggers a quiet but persistent fear: what happens if I get sick? That fear is understandable. In the United States, healthcare is not merely a service; it is an economic hazard. Insurance premiums rise unpredictably, deductibles reset annually, and even insured patients can face staggering bills from providers they never chose. Medical care is often excellent, but access to it feels contingent, fragile, and adversarial.

This experience shapes how Americans think about health. Care is delayed because it is expensive. Treatment decisions are filtered through cost rather than need. Insurance becomes something to defend rather than rely on. Over time, this produces a mentality grounded in caution and mistrust, one in which illness is not just a physical event but a financial threat.

Bob, a retired airline pilot, carried this mindset with him when he and his wife, Beryl, moved to the Greek island of Santorini after decades of flying internationally for a global airline. Retirement had been active and purposeful: board service, philanthropy, and the satisfaction of finally living in a place he had once only overflown. But when Bob began experiencing chest pains, the limits of island medicine became suddenly clear. The local clinic could not manage the emergency, and he was evacuated by helicopter to Athens, where advanced care was available. The transfer narrowly saved his life. What made the difference was not the quality of Greek medicine, but the existence of a system that anticipated escalation—and the reality that such escalation required leaving the island entirely.

When Americans move abroad, their attitudes about healthcare travel with them, shaping assumptions about risk and coverage long after the surrounding systems have changed. Many new expats are stunned to discover that routine medical visits cost less than a co-pay back home, that imaging and lab work are priced transparently, and that doctors often spend more time with patients. Yet this initial relief can be dangerous if it leads to complacency. Lower cost does not eliminate the need for coverage, and accessibility does not replace the requirement for legal eligibility.

The first and most important lesson of healthcare abroad is that the existence of quality care and formal access to it are not the same. Being physically in a country does not mean being part of its healthcare system. Many countries offer excellent healthcare infrastructure, but it is designed to serve citizens and legally registered residents, not visitors who happen to be present. Coverage is earned, purchased, or granted through status.

This distinction is where many Americans misstep. Accustomed to a system in which insurance is portable within national borders, they assume that presence alone creates entitlement. Abroad, healthcare is inseparable from immigration status. Residency permits, visa categories, and insurance policies determine not only what care you can receive, but how and at what cost. Without proper planning, even the best system can become inaccessible precisely when it is needed most.

Compounding this confusion is the fact that Medicare, the backbone of healthcare for older Americans, does not travel. Medicare coverage generally stops at the U.S. border, with only narrow and rare exceptions. For retirees accustomed to viewing Medicare as a safety net, this reality can feel destabilizing. Some attempt to rely on informal care or out-of-pocket payment abroad, underestimating how quickly costs can escalate in emergencies or during prolonged illness. Others assume they will simply return to the United States for care, overlooking the logistical and financial barriers that illness itself may impose.

The result is a gap between perception and preparedness. Americans often underestimate how central healthcare planning is to a successful life abroad. Housing can be changed. Location can be adjusted. Visas can sometimes be modified. But illness collapses flexibility, forcing immediate interaction with systems that do not bend to improvisation. Healthcare planning must precede emigration, not follow it.

One of the most striking differences Americans encounter abroad is the normalization of private medical insurance as a residency requirement rather than a discretionary purchase. In many countries, proof of comprehensive health insurance is required to obtain a long-term visa. This insurance must often meet specific criteria: full coverage, no significant exclusions, validity within the host country, and sometimes the absence of deductibles or co-payments. Travel insurance, no matter how generous it appears, is frequently rejected because it is designed for emergencies, not for residence.

This requirement reflects a fundamental policy logic. Insurance is not merely protection for the individual; it is a guarantee to the state. Host countries expect newcomers to arrive self-sufficient, capable of meeting their healthcare needs without burdening public systems. For Americans, this reframes insurance from a personal hedge into a civic obligation tied directly to legal presence.

Understanding this shift is essential. Healthcare abroad is not chaotic or risky by default, but it is conditional. The condition is planning. Those who approach healthcare as an afterthought often find themselves scrambling, purchasing inadequate policies, or facing visa delays and denials. Those who treat healthcare as foundational—equal in importance to housing and legal status—experience far fewer disruptions.

Equally important is the recognition that healthcare abroad is not monolithic. Systems vary in structure, funding, and access rules, but they share a common principle: entitlement flows from contribution or compliance. No system assumes coverage by default: public systems generally require residency and registration, private systems require payment or insurance. For Americans used to employer-sponsored insurance or automatic Medicare enrollment, this shift requires unlearning deeply ingrained expectations.

Yet once this unlearning occurs, many expats report a profound sense of relief. Healthcare becomes legible. Costs are known. Insurance policies are readable. Providers are accessible. The adversarial tone that characterizes so much of American healthcare fades, replaced by a more transactional but less hostile relationship. Care is no longer mediated primarily through billing departments and coding disputes. It is delivered directly, often simply, and frequently at a fraction of the cost.

This does not mean that healthcare abroad is perfect or universally superior. Delays exist. Language barriers matter. Rural access may be limited. But for Americans who plan properly, the overall experience is often less stressful and more humane. The key is recognizing that this outcome is not accidental. It is the result of aligning immigration status, insurance coverage, and realistic expectations before a crisis occurs.

Part II: Coverage, Compliance, and the Architecture of Care

Once Americans understand that healthcare abroad is inseparable from legal status, the next question becomes practical rather than philosophical: how, exactly, does coverage work? This is where assumptions formed in the U.S. system most often collide with reality. In America, insurance is layered, opaque, and frequently tied to employment. Abroad, healthcare coverage is usually simpler—but also far less forgiving of misunderstanding.

The most important distinction is between access and eligibility. Access refers to the physical presence of hospitals, clinics, and doctors. Eligibility refers to the right to use them under specific financial terms. Many Americans conflate the two, assuming that because care is available, it is also affordable or covered. In reality, eligibility depends almost entirely on whether you have enrolled properly in a system—public or private—or whether you are insured in a way the host country recognizes.

For most Americans living abroad, especially in the first years, private health insurance is the cornerstone of this eligibility. It is not a luxury product or a temporary bridge. It is the mechanism through which residence itself becomes possible. Many long-term visas explicitly require proof of comprehensive private insurance before approval, and some continue to require it at renewal. This insurance must usually be valid locally, renewable, and free of major exclusions. The policy is examined not as a financial instrument but as a compliance document.

This often surprises Americans who assume that lower healthcare costs make insurance optional. It is true that out-of-pocket care abroad is often inexpensive by U.S. standards, but cost alone does not substitute for coverage. Emergencies, hospitalization, and chronic conditions can escalate quickly. More importantly, immigration authorities are not concerned with whether you can afford today's care, but whether you have arranged for tomorrow's.

Private international insurance fills this gap by creating portability and predictability. These policies are designed for people who live outside their home country, often covering care across multiple jurisdictions. They differ from travel insurance in critical ways. Travel insurance assumes short stays and emergency-only scenarios. It often excludes routine care, ongoing treatment, and pre-existing conditions. International health insurance, by contrast, is structured for residence and covers primary care, specialist visits, hospitalization, and often prescriptions. It is renewable annually, which is essential for visa continuity.

Choosing such insurance requires careful attention. Coverage limits, geographic scope, deductibles, and exclusions vary widely. Some policies exclude the United States entirely, lowering premiums significantly but eliminating coverage if you return home. Others include global coverage at a higher cost. For Americans who plan to move frequently or return periodically, these distinctions matter. Insurance becomes part of lifestyle design rather than a passive purchase.

Age also plays a role. Younger expats often focus on affordability, opting for higher deductibles or narrower coverage. Older expats, particularly retirees, may prioritize stability and access, accepting higher premiums in exchange for comprehensive care. Pre-existing conditions introduce further complexity. Some insurers exclude them entirely; others cover them after waiting periods or at increased cost. Transparency is essential. Failing to disclose medical history can void coverage precisely when it is needed most.

Public healthcare systems enter the picture later, usually after residency is established. Many countries allow legal residents to enroll in public systems after registration, contribution, or a probationary period. This process varies, but the principle is consistent: public healthcare is tied to integration. Taxes, social contributions, or fixed fees create entitlement. Until that entitlement is formalized, private insurance remains mandatory.

Even after public enrollment, many expats maintain private coverage. Public systems are often excellent, but demand can create delays for non-urgent care. Private insurance offers speed, choice, and continuity, particularly in urban centers. The coexistence of public and private care is not a failure of the system but a feature. It allows individuals to calibrate access according to need and preference. For Americans accustomed to binary debates about public versus private healthcare, this hybrid model can feel refreshingly pragmatic.

Another critical element of coverage abroad is emergency planning. Serious illness or injury can create situations that exceed local capacity or personal comfort. Medical evacuation insurance addresses this risk, covering transport to another facility or country when necessary. Without such coverage, evacuation costs can be catastrophic. Many comprehensive international policies include evacuation and repatriation automatically; others require riders or separate policies. This detail is often overlooked until it is too late.

Prescription coverage also requires adjustment. Medications that are expensive or tightly controlled in the United States may be inexpensive and widely available abroad. Conversely, some drugs common in the U.S. may be unavailable or prescribed differently. Insurance policies vary in how they handle prescriptions, particularly for long-term conditions. Expats must learn to navigate formularies, generic equivalents, and local prescribing practices. This learning curve can be steep initially, but often results in lower costs and fewer barriers over time.

Language and administration shape the experience as well. Even in countries with strong healthcare systems, navigating them without local language skills can be intimidating. Insurance providers that offer multilingual support, direct billing, and local assistance reduce this friction dramatically. The value of such support is often underestimated until an urgent situation arises. Good insurance does more than reimburse costs; it mediates access.

Healthcare abroad rewards intentional structure. Those who assemble coverage thoughtfully—aligning insurance, residency, and realistic use patterns—experience healthcare as one of the most reassuring aspects of life overseas. Those who rely on assumptions or improvisation often experience it as a source of anxiety. In this sense, healthcare abroad mirrors the broader logic of emigration itself. Stability is available, but it must be constructed deliberately. Understanding that is essential for anyone seeking not just to live abroad, but to live well.

Part III: Health, Aging, and Long-Term Security

For Americans living abroad, the true test of any healthcare arrangement is not how it performs during routine visits or minor illnesses, but how it holds up over time. Acute care is episodic; aging is cumulative. Chronic conditions, mobility changes, mental health, and end-of-life planning slowly move from abstraction to inevitability. Emigration does not pause this trajectory. It alters the environment in which it unfolds.

One of the most important shifts expats experience is the redefinition of what "security" means in healthcare. In the United States, security is often equated with brand names—large hospital systems, familiar insurers, renowned specialists—even when access to those systems is financially precarious. Abroad, security tends to be structural rather than reputational. It lies in predictability: knowing what care costs, how to access it, and who is responsible for payment. For many expats, this clarity proves more reassuring than the promise of elite care that may be financially out of reach.

As years pass, the importance of continuity becomes more pronounced. Managing chronic conditions abroad requires more than good doctors; it requires stable insurance, consistent access to medication, and reliable administrative processes. This is where in-country insurance—or internationally portable insurance with local compliance—shows its real value. Policies designed for residence allow ongoing treatment, regular monitoring, and relationship-based care. They transform healthcare from a contingency plan into an integrated part of daily life.

Mental health deserves particular attention. Relocating abroad, even under positive circumstances, is stressful. Language barriers, cultural adjustment, distance from family, and identity shifts can quietly erode well-being. While mental health care is widely available in many countries, access often depends on insurance coverage and cultural norms. Expats who plan only for physical health sometimes discover too late that counseling, psychiatric care, or medication management is harder to access without proper coverage or local referrals. Comprehensive insurance that includes mental health services is not indulgent; it is preventive care.

Aging abroad also forces earlier confrontation with questions Americans often postpone. What happens if independence declines? Who assists with daily tasks? How are long-term care needs addressed? In the U.S., these questions are often deferred until crisis, at which point options narrow rapidly. Abroad, the absence of default systems like Medicare-funded post-acute care makes planning even more critical. Some expats choose locations with strong family-oriented cultures or affordable in-home care. Others maintain flexible arrangements that allow relocation as needs change. What matters is not finding a perfect solution, but acknowledging that healthcare planning does not end with insurance enrollment.

For some Americans, the question eventually arises whether to return to the United States for advanced care. This is not a failure of the host country's system, nor is it uncommon. Many expats maintain the option to seek care in multiple places, depending on circumstances. The critical factor is not where care occurs, but whether access is planned or improvised. Insurance that allows treatment in more than one country, or a strategy that preserves some level of U.S. healthcare access, provides flexibility without dependence.

Another often overlooked consideration is medical decision-making authority. Advance directives, powers of attorney, and living wills do not always transfer cleanly across borders. Laws governing consent, guardianship, and end-of-life care vary. Expats who take time to align legal documents with local frameworks spare themselves and their families confusion during moments of vulnerability. This is not morbid: it is an extension of the same intentionality and preparation that make emigration sustainable in the first place.

Healthcare abroad rewards those who treat it as infrastructure rather than insurance alone. It is a system composed of legal status, coverage, providers, language, and contingency planning. Remove one element and the structure weakens. Assemble them thoughtfully, and healthcare becomes one of the most stabilizing aspects of life overseas.

This realization reframes the initial surprise many Americans feel when encountering affordable care abroad. The true benefit is not cost savings, though those are real. It is the restoration of proportionality. Healthcare becomes something to manage, not to fear. Decisions are guided by need rather than panic. Illness is addressed directly rather than deferred. For many expats, this shift alone justifies the effort required to plan properly. Freed from constant financial anxiety around care, they become more attentive to health itself. Preventive visits feel reasonable. Follow-ups happen on time. Wellness becomes part of life rather than an aspirational ideal. In a quieter way than any change of scenery, this may be the most profound transformation of all.

Chapter 9

SCHOOLS, STABILITY & STORYBOOKS

RAISING CHILDREN ABROAD

Part I: When the Decision Is No Longer Just Yours

Navigating all aspects of building a life abroad—visas and residency, banking and taxes, housing and healthcare—is something everyone making the move must consider. Those with school-age children must consider all this and more. Education sits at the center of this project. School is not merely a place of learning; it is the primary arena in which children build friendships, absorb cultural norms, and develop confidence. Abroad, schooling choices shape not only academic outcomes but also social integration and language acquisition. The question is not simply which system is best, but which is best for this family, at this moment, with these children.

For some families, the most consequential educational decisions are not about primary school at all, but about timing. Bill and Michelle Peterson learned this the hard way. They moved from California with their seventeen-year-old son, Jason, to what they considered their ideal village near Lyon, France—a place they had dreamed about for years. For Bill and Michelle, the move represented freedom, beauty, and a long-delayed transition into the life they had imagined after raising a family. For Jason, it felt different.

Jason finished high school in France, adapted well enough, and did what was asked of him. But his sense of home remained firmly anchored in California. When it came time for college, he wanted to return to the United States and attend school in his hometown. That was when the unintended consequences surfaced. Because the Petersons had already sold their California home and established residency abroad, Jason no longer qualified for in-state tuition. The family suddenly faced more than $300,000 in tuition and related expenses—costs that could have been largely avoided had they waited just one year before making the move.

Nothing about the Petersons' decision was reckless. They planned carefully, chose thoughtfully, and prioritized family well-being. What they underestimated was how rigid some systems remain, even in an otherwise flexible world. Residency rules do not bend easily, and education finance is one of the least forgiving domains of all. The lesson was not that the move was a mistake, but that sequencing matters. When children are nearing educational thresholds, a single year can carry outsized financial and emotional consequences.

Education abroad is deeply contextual, shaped by residency status, language proficiency, length of stay, and family resources. Some families prioritize continuity, choosing schools that mirror American curricula to ensure smooth transitions. Others embrace immersion, viewing local schools as the gateway to cultural integration and linguistic fluency. Still others adopt hybrid approaches, combining formal schooling with online education or homeschooling to preserve flexibility.

What unites successful families is not a particular choice, but intentionality. They research extensively, visit schools in person when possible, and remain open to adjustment. They understand that the first choice may not be the final one, and that adaptation is part of the process rather than a sign of failure. Education abroad is not a static decision; it evolves as children grow and circumstances change.

Children themselves often surprise their parents. Younger children, in particular, tend to adapt with remarkable speed. Language acquisition happens organically through play and routine. Social barriers dissolve quickly when children share classrooms, games, and rituals. What adults perceive as daunting—new languages, unfamiliar customs—children often experience as normal. For them, the world simply is the world they are given.

Older children and teenagers face a more complex adjustment. Identity formation intensifies during adolescence, and being different can be uncomfortable. Language barriers may feel more frustrating. Academic alignment becomes more consequential as graduation requirements and college pathways come into view. Yet even here, outcomes are not predetermined. With appropriate support—and with careful attention to timing—many older children emerge more self-aware, resilient, and globally fluent than their peers who never leave home.

Parents, too, undergo transformation. Raising children abroad forces adults to relinquish some control. They cannot mediate every interaction or translate every experience. Children become cultural intermediaries, sometimes mastering language and norms faster than their parents. This reversal can feel unsettling, but it often strengthens family bonds. Parents learn alongside their children, modeling curiosity and humility rather than authority alone.

Healthcare and safety inevitably enter the conversation as well. Parents need reassurance that their children will be cared for if something goes wrong. Abroad, pediatric care is often excellent and accessible, but eligibility depends on residency and insurance. Families who plan carefully find that healthcare becomes one of the most reassuring aspects of life overseas. Children receive routine care without the financial anxiety that shadows so many American families.

Beyond the logistics of school choice and healthcare lies the deeper question of culture. Raising children abroad means raising them between worlds: traditions shift, holidays are celebrated differently, and norms around discipline, independence, and social behavior vary. Children absorb these differences intuitively, often moving fluidly between cultural contexts. Over time, many develop a sense of identity that is additive rather than exclusive. They do not lose their American identity; they layer it with others.

This layering is one of the most enduring gifts of an international childhood. Children raised abroad tend to develop a broader sense of possibility. They learn early that ways of living are choices rather than inevitabilities. They see that systems can be organized differently and that language shapes perception. These insights are difficult to teach abstractly, but lived experience makes them tangible.

None of this diminishes the challenges. There will be moments of loneliness, frustration, and doubt—for children and parents alike. Raising children abroad is not about creating a perfect childhood. It is about creating a meaningful one. It asks parents to think expansively about education, stability, and belonging. It requires more planning, communication, and flexibility than raising children within familiar systems. But for many, the reward is profound: children who grow up with confidence in difference, comfort in transition, and a sense that the world is larger—and more navigable—than they were ever taught to believe.

Part II: Learning Between Worlds

Once a family commits to life abroad, education becomes the axis around which nearly every other decision turns. Where a child goes to school determines daily rhythms, language exposure, social circles, and long-term mobility. It shapes how quickly a family integrates and how deeply children come to feel that a place is home. For parents, schooling abroad is not simply about academic quality, but alignment between values, expectations, and the lived reality of childhood.

One of the first realizations parents encounter is that education abroad is less standardized than in the United States. There is no single national narrative about what school should be or what success looks like. Instead, education reflects cultural priorities. In some places, structure and discipline are emphasized. In others, autonomy and creativity take precedence. Homework loads, testing regimes, and teacher-student relationships vary widely. This diversity can feel disorienting, particularly for American parents accustomed to benchmarking schools against familiar metrics.

International schools often appear the safest entry point, offering continuity in language and curriculum, easing transitions, and preserving academic portability. For families expecting to move again, or those with older children approaching college age, this continuity can be invaluable. Children can step into classrooms that resemble what they left behind, minimizing disruption during an already significant life change. Socially, international schools provide instant community among peers who are also navigating cross-cultural lives.

Yet this familiarity comes at a cost, both financial and experiential. International schools can be expensive, sometimes rivaling private education in the United States. More subtly, they can insulate children from the surrounding culture. Days unfold in English, friendships are formed within expatriate circles, and local life remains something observed rather than lived. For some families, this insulation is intentional and appropriate. For others, it feels like a missed opportunity.

Local schools represent the opposite end of the spectrum. They immerse children fully in the language, customs, and social fabric of the host community. Young children, in particular, often thrive in this environment, acquiring fluency and cultural intuition with astonishing speed. For parents committed to long-term residence and integration, local schools can anchor a family's life abroad more powerfully than any other institution.

This immersion, however, requires patience and trust. The early months can be challenging, as children struggle to express themselves, fall behind academically while adjusting linguistically, or feel socially adrift. Parents must resist the urge to interpret temporary discomfort as permanent harm. With support and time, many children not only catch up but surpass expectations, developing cognitive flexibility and resilience that serve them well throughout life.

Between these two poles lies a wide range of hybrid options. Private local schools may offer bilingual instruction or alternative pedagogies that blend national curricula with international perspectives. Online schooling and homeschooling appeal to families seeking flexibility, particularly those who move frequently or live in areas where local options are limited. These approaches allow parents to tailor education closely to their children's needs, but they also demand greater parental involvement and careful attention to legal requirements.

What becomes clear is that no schooling choice is neutral. Each carries tradeoffs that intersect with family priorities. Academic rigor may come at the expense of social integration. Cultural immersion may complicate future transitions. Flexibility may require greater structure at home. Successful families do not eliminate these tradeoffs; they choose which ones they are willing to manage.

Language, not merely a tool for communication but a gateway to belonging, sits at the heart of these decisions. Those who gain fluency early often report feeling more at ease, more confident, and more invested in their surroundings. Language acquisition also reshapes family dynamics. Children may become translators for parents, reversing traditional hierarchies of competence. This shift can be empowering for children and humbling for adults, fostering mutual dependence rather than unilateral authority.

Parents who commit to learning the local language alongside their children often find integration smoother and family cohesion stronger. Language becomes a shared project rather than a burden placed solely on young shoulders. It signals respect for the host culture and models lifelong learning. Even imperfect attempts can open doors socially, signaling willingness rather than mastery.

Academic transitions require careful navigation as well. Curriculum differences can create gaps or redundancies when children move between systems. Subjects may be introduced earlier or later than expected. Teaching styles may clash with prior habits. Parents who plan ahead—maintaining records, understanding equivalencies, and anticipating future transitions—reduce stress when moves occur. Yet even with planning, some friction is inevitable. Adaptability is as important as preparation.

Social development unfolds alongside academics. School is where children learn not only math and reading, but how to navigate relationships, resolve conflict, and understand social norms. Abroad, these lessons are amplified, as children encounter different expectations around behavior, authority, and friendship. They learn quickly that rules are culturally contingent rather than universal. This awareness can be confusing initially, but it often fosters empathy and social intelligence.

Friendships formed abroad may feel intense, shaped by shared vulnerability and transience. Children learn to connect quickly and to say goodbye gracefully. While this can be emotionally taxing, it also builds skills rarely cultivated in more static environments. Many internationally raised children develop an ease with transition and a capacity for deep connection that belies their age.

At the same time, parents must remain attentive to signs of distress. Not all children adapt at the same pace or in the same way. Language frustration, academic pressure, or social isolation can accumulate quietly. Open communication within the family is essential. Regular check-ins, validation of mixed feelings, and access to support—whether through school counselors or external professionals—help children process their experiences constructively.

Education abroad is not a single decision but an ongoing negotiation. Families reassess as children grow, as residency plans evolve, and as priorities shift. What works at age five may not work at fifteen. Flexibility, rather than perfection, is the key.

Part III: Belonging, Identity, and the Long View

Beyond classrooms and curricula lies the deeper work of raising children abroad: helping them develop a sense of belonging in a world that may never feel singular or fixed. Education structures daily life, but identity is shaped in quieter spaces—in neighborhoods, playgrounds, family routines, and the stories children tell themselves about who they are and where they come from. For families living internationally, this dimension of childhood is both the most fragile and the most transformative.

One of the first tensions parents encounter is the balance between continuity and change. Children need anchors—rituals, relationships, and expectations that provide emotional security. At the same time, an international life introduces constant novelty. New languages, customs, and social cues can invigorate curiosity but also exhaust it. Families who thrive abroad are often those who create islands of familiarity within a sea of difference. Family meals, bedtime routines, shared holidays, and regular communication with extended family become stabilizing forces. These rituals signal to children that while surroundings may change, the core of family life remains intact.

Social integration plays a decisive role. Friendships are the currency of childhood, and access to them determines whether a place feels welcoming or alienating. Some children find their footing quickly, drawn into local games and social circles with little hesitation. Others struggle, particularly when language barriers or cultural differences make them feel conspicuous. Parents must tread carefully, offering support without over management. Intervening too aggressively can undermine confidence; withdrawing too completely can leave children isolated. The art lies in being present, observant, and responsive.

Expat communities often provide an initial refuge. Shared language and experiences can ease the transition and offer parents much-needed support. Yet remaining exclusively within these circles carries risks. Children may internalize a sense of separateness, perceiving themselves as temporary guests rather than participants in local life. Families who find a balance—maintaining expat connections while encouraging local engagement—tend to foster more resilient identities. Children learn that they can belong in multiple spaces without being confined to any single one.

Healthcare, too, intersects with belonging in subtle ways. For children, access to consistent medical and mental health care reinforces a sense of safety. Knowing where to go when sick, recognizing familiar providers, and understanding how systems work all contribute to stability. Parents who ensure comprehensive in-country health insurance and establish care early often find that this practical preparation has emotional dividends, reducing anxiety during inevitable childhood illnesses and reinforcing trust in the new environment.

Legal and logistical considerations quietly shape children's experiences as well. Residency permits, school enrollment rules, and documentation requirements can influence how rooted a child feels. Being legally recognized—registered at school, enrolled in health systems, included in local activities—signals legitimacy. Children are acutely sensitive to cues about whether they truly "belong" somewhere. Parents who handle these details proactively spare their children the stress of feeling provisional or invisible.

Identity formation unfolds differently for children raised across borders. Many develop a sort of layered identity, drawing from multiple cultures without feeling wholly defined by any one of them. This can be a source of strength, fostering adaptability and empathy; it can also generate confusion, particularly during adolescence, when questions of belonging intensify. "Where are you from?" becomes a complex question with no simple answer. Families who create space for these conversations—acknowledging ambiguity rather than resolving it prematurely—help children integrate their experiences into a coherent sense of self.

There are losses, and it is important not to minimize them. Children may miss grandparents, childhood friends, or cultural reference points that peers take for granted. They may feel out of sync when returning to the United States, no longer fully aligned with the assumptions of their passport country. These feelings are real and deserve recognition. Yet loss and gain are not opposites; they coexist. Many internationally raised children carry nostalgia alongside gratitude, longing alongside confidence.

Looking back, families who have raised children abroad often describe the experience less in terms of outcomes and more in terms of perspective. Their children tend to approach difference with curiosity rather than fear. They navigate uncertainty with greater ease. They understand, intuitively, that the world is not organized around a single norm. These qualities do not guarantee success or happiness, but they provide tools for navigating an increasingly interconnected and unpredictable world.

For parents, the journey reshapes assumptions about control and protection. Raising children abroad requires trust—in systems that are not fully understood, in children's capacity to adapt, and in one's own ability to respond thoughtfully when challenges arise. It also requires humility. Parents learn alongside their children, making mistakes, revising plans, and sometimes acknowledging that what seemed right at one stage no longer serves at another.

In the end, raising children abroad is not about producing global citizens in a superficial sense. It is about expanding the range of experiences through which children learn to understand themselves and others. Choosing to raise children abroad is among the most consequential decisions a family can make. It is a decision that carries risk, demands preparation, and invites uncertainty. It also offers something rare: the chance to raise children who see the world not as a map divided by borders, but as a place of stories, connections, and possibilities waiting to be discovered.

Chapter 10

LIFESTYLE DESIGN & QUALITY OF LIFE

Part I: After the Paperwork, the Living

Richard, a retired American corporate executive, and his wife Sofia, a still-working corporate finance professional, believed they had designed the ideal transition to living abroad. They purchased a house in a historic village in Tuscany—an area Sofia knew well. She had been born nearby, spoke flawless Italian, and was deeply familiar with local customs, norms, and social codes. This was not a romanticized fantasy of Italy; it was a return, or so it seemed.

From the outside, their plan appeared airtight: cultural fluency, linguistic competency, family roots, financial stability. And yet, life inside the village unfolded very differently than expected.

Despite Sofia's background, the couple remained outsiders. Social acceptance never materialized. Routine tasks—repairs, renovations, basic work on the house—became unexpectedly difficult, slowed not by bureaucracy but quiet resistance. Local contractors were unresponsive. Informal networks remained closed. Sofia was judged for her life choices: for having built a career abroad, for marrying an American, for not having children, for being perceived as too modern, too independent, too removed from the village's expectations of womanhood and continuity.

Belonging, they learned, is not conferred by ancestry or language alone. It is negotiated through conformity, patience, and often through life choices made decades earlier. Sofia's sophistication—which had served her well professionally and culturally elsewhere—worked against her here, and the life they had envisioned—grounded, graceful, restorative—never took shape.

Eventually, Richard and Sofia made the difficult decision to abandon the attempt, sell the property, and relocate to the United Kingdom. There was no dramatic failure, no single moment of rupture—just the slow realization that quality of life is not determined by beauty, history, or even cultural familiarity, but by whether daily life feels workable, dignified, and humane.

Their experience illustrates a truth many expatriates learn only through trial: lifestyle fit is not the same as cultural alignment. One can love a country, speak its language, and admire its traditions—and still not be able to live comfortably within its social structure. Quality of life depends as much on informal acceptance as on formal legality.

This is why expatriation is not merely a change of address. It is a lifestyle choice in the deepest sense. It asks fundamental questions: What is enough? What deserves my time? What do I want my days to feel like, not just my years?

One of the earliest confrontations facing expatriates is pace. In many parts of the world, life moves more slowly—not inefficiently, but deliberately. Meals are longer. Bureaucracy takes time. Social interactions are less transactional. For Americans trained to equate speed with competence and convenience with success, this can feel uncomfortable, even irritating. Waiting becomes unavoidable. Plans unfold gradually. Immediate gratification is often unavailable.

Some expatriates interpret this as frustration. Others experience it as relief.

Those who thrive stop fighting the tempo and begin listening to it. They learn that time abroad is structured less around productivity and more around continuity. Days are meant to be lived fully rather than conquered efficiently. The shift is subtle but profound. When time is no longer constantly monetized, it becomes available for attention—for walking, talking, cooking, noticing.

There is a moment every expatriate reaches that no checklist can prepare them for. The visa has been approved. The bank account exists. Healthcare is arranged. Children are enrolled, or plans are in place. The adrenaline that carried the move forward finally dissipates. The emails stop. The forms are filed. And then, quietly, life begins.

This is the moment when expatriation stops being a project and becomes a presence. It is no longer about permissions or plans, but about how each day actually unfolds. How you wake up. How you move through space. How you eat, rest, connect, and think. The question is no longer whether you can live abroad, but whether you know how to live well there.

Many Americans arrive overseas carrying an unexamined assumption: that quality of life will automatically improve simply by changing geography. And often, it does—at least initially. The novelty of a new place can feel intoxicating. Walkable streets replace traffic jams. Cafés replace drive-throughs. The pace slows. The air feels lighter. Life seems, for a time, more humane.

But novelty fades. What remains is rhythm. And rhythm, not scenery, determines whether a life feels nourishing or hollow.

Lifestyle design is the unglamorous but essential work of shaping that rhythm. It requires honesty about what truly matters, rather than what looks good in photographs or sounds appealing in conversation. It asks not what kind of life you admire, but what kind of life you can actually inhabit day after day.

For many Americans, this is unfamiliar territory. Life in the United States is often reactive rather than intentional, structured around work demands, commuting patterns, consumption cycles, and institutional schedules. Time is fragmented. Space is optimized for efficiency rather than presence. Relationships are frequently squeezed into margins. When Americans move abroad, they are given an unusual opportunity: to reconstruct daily life from the ground up.

But opportunity cuts both ways. Without the scaffolding of familiar systems, expatriates must decide what fills the empty spaces. If they do not choose deliberately, old habits rush in to occupy new settings. The same stress patterns, the same over-scheduling, the same pursuit of convenience can quietly reassert themselves—only now without the cultural context that once made them feel normal.

Transportation often becomes the first tangible expression of this shift. In much of the world, daily life does not revolve around private vehicles. Walking, public transit, cycling, and shared mobility dominate. Distances shrink when they are measured in minutes rather than miles. Errands become encounters. Movement becomes part of life rather than something endured between destinations.

This physical reorientation affects mental health in ways many expatriates do not anticipate. Walking more means noticing more. Streets become familiar. Neighborhoods develop texture. The body moves differently, and the mind follows. Even those who initially resist giving up car-centric habits often find that once they do, their relationship to space and time changes permanently.

Housing reinforces this recalibration. American homes often emphasize size, storage, and separation. Abroad, living spaces tend to be smaller, denser, and closer to daily life. Walls are thicker. Rooms are multifunctional. Outdoor space is shared or public rather than private. This compression can feel like a loss at first, particularly for those accustomed to square footage as a measure of success.

Over time, many expatriates experience it as liberation. Less space demands less maintenance. Fewer possessions require less management. Life expands outward into cafés, parks, plazas, and streets rather than inward into rooms filled with things. The boundary between private and public life softens. Community becomes something encountered, not scheduled.

Food is often where lifestyle change is most viscerally felt. Abroad, eating is less about convenience and more about rhythm. Markets replace megastores. Seasonal availability dictates menus. Meals are social events rather than refueling stops. Portions are smaller, but attention is greater. Cooking becomes a daily practice rather than a weekend project.

For Americans accustomed to abundance as default, this shift can feel restrictive. Yet many find that their relationship to food becomes healthier without conscious effort. Eating slows. Taste sharpens. Waste decreases. Meals anchor the day, creating natural pauses that structure time. The body adjusts, and so does the mind.

Leisure follows a similar pattern. In many cultures, rest is not something earned after exhaustion but something integrated into daily life. Afternoons slow. Evenings stretch. Public holidays are observed collectively rather than squeezed between obligations. For expatriates, this can feel disorienting at first. Without constant busyness, the question arises, "What do I do with myself?"

This is where lifestyle design becomes existential. Living abroad removes many external pressures but offers no automatic sense of meaning. That must be cultivated. Some expatriates fill the space with travel, moving constantly in search of stimulation. Others retreat into isolation, overwhelmed by choice. Those who find contentment tend to do something simpler: they let life become ordinary again.

Ordinary, in this context, does not mean dull. It means grounded. It means learning the local bakery's hours. Greeting the same neighbors. Returning to the same café. Developing routines that are small but reliable. Meaning emerges not from constant novelty but from familiarity deepened over time.

The paradox of expatriate life is that while it begins with dramatic change, it ultimately depends on acceptance of the mundane. A life abroad that feels sustainable is one that no longer feels exotic. It feels lived-in. It feels like yours.

Part II: Relationships, Belonging, and the Texture of Daily Life

If transportation, housing, and food determine the shape of daily life abroad, relationships determine its depth. No amount of walkability or café culture can compensate for isolation. Quality of life is ultimately relational. It is measured not only by how pleasant a place is, but by whether one feels seen, known, and connected within it.

For many Americans, this is the most underestimated challenge of living abroad. In the United States, social life is often structured around institutions—workplaces, schools, religious communities, and organized activities. When those structures fall away, connection must be built intentionally rather than assumed. Living abroad exposes how much of one's social world was once automatic, and how much now requires effort.

Early on, expatriates often gravitate toward other foreigners. Shared language and shared displacement create instant familiarity. Expat communities can provide practical support, emotional validation, and a sense of continuity during the transition period. But expat friendships are often transient. People arrive and depart. Visas expire. Life circumstances change. Bonds can be intense but short-lived. While this fluidity can be enriching, it can also feel destabilizing over time. Those who rely exclusively on expat circles may find themselves repeatedly rebuilding their social world, never quite settling into a sense of permanence.

Local relationships, by contrast, tend to develop slowly. In many cultures, friendships are not formed quickly or casually. Trust is built through repetition, presence, and shared history rather than immediate openness. Americans accustomed to friendliness as a social norm may misinterpret reserve as rejection. In reality, it is often a different pacing of intimacy rather than an absence of warmth.

Learning to adapt to this pacing is one of the most important acts of cultural translation an expatriate can undertake. It requires patience and humility. Relationships are not formed through networking or efficiency, but through consistency. Returning to the same places. Participating in the same routines. Showing up without agenda. Over time, familiarity accumulates, and with it, trust.

Language plays a decisive role here. Even basic efforts to speak the local language signal respect and commitment. Fluency is less important than willingness: a greeting offered imperfectly often opens more doors than silence delivered flawlessly. Language learning becomes not just a practical tool but a social gesture, one that communicates a desire to belong rather than merely to consume.

Many expatriates experience a subtle identity shift as relationships deepen. They are no longer defined primarily by what they do or where they came from, but by how they participate. The absence of familiar status markers—job titles, professional networks, social shorthand—levels the field. People are encountered more directly, less mediated by resumes or assumptions. For some, this is liberating; for others, it is disorienting.

This disorientation is part of the work. Living abroad strips away inherited identities and invites new ones to form. It asks expatriates to consider who they are when no one knows their backstory. Relationships become mirrors that reflect behavior rather than biography. Over time, many find that this leads to a quieter, more grounded sense of self.

Community engagement often becomes the bridge between isolation and belonging. This does not require grand gestures. Small acts—joining a local class, volunteering, attending neighborhood events, participating in shared rituals—create points of contact. These interactions may feel insignificant at first, but they accumulate. Presence, repeated over time, transforms anonymity into recognition.

Family dynamics shift as well. Couples who move abroad together often find that their relationship intensifies. Without the distractions of familiar social networks, partners rely more heavily on one another. This can strengthen bonds, but it can also expose fractures. Successful expatriate couples tend to cultivate individual lives alongside shared ones, allowing each partner space to form connections and routines independent of the relationship.

For those raising children, schools often become the primary social interface. Through school communities, parents meet other families. Children's friendships pull adults into new social worlds. These connections can anchor families in place, providing continuity even as other aspects of life change.

Loneliness, however, is not uncommon, particularly in the first year. The effort required to build relationships abroad is real, and progress can feel slow. Many expatriates experience a period of emotional flatness after the initial excitement fades. This is not a sign of failure but a normal stage of adjustment. Recognizing it as such prevents premature conclusions about the move itself.

What distinguishes those who settle from those who leave is often not the absence of loneliness, but the willingness to move through it. Those who remain open, who continue showing up despite awkwardness or fatigue, eventually find that connection emerges quietly, often when least expected. Belonging is rarely announced. It is felt gradually, through small recognitions and shared moments.

Over time, daily life acquires texture. Familiar faces appear on morning walks. Conversations deepen. Rituals form. The place that once felt foreign becomes layered with personal meaning. This transformation does not require full assimilation or the abandonment of one's original culture. It requires participation. Belonging is not about becoming someone else; it is about being present where you are.

In this way, lifestyle design abroad becomes an exercise in relational awareness. Quality of life is not achieved through optimization alone. It emerges from connection—from the willingness to be changed by place as much as to choose it.

Part III: Meaning, Enough, and the Quiet Success of a Life Well Lived

At some point, if expatriation endures, a subtle shift occurs. The questions that once dominated—How do I set this up? How does this system work? Do I belong here?—begin to fade into the background. Daily life acquires familiarity. The streets are known. The language, even if imperfect, is usable. Routines take hold. And in that settling, a deeper question emerges, one that has little to do with logistics and everything to do with meaning.

What am I doing here—really?

This is the moment when lifestyle design moves beyond optimization and becomes existential. Living abroad no longer feels like an experiment or an escape. It becomes a mirror, reflecting the choices one makes when stripped of familiar pressures and expectations. Without the constant urgency of American life—the default scripts of productivity, consumption, and status—expatriates are left with something rare: space to decide what matters.

For some, this space is initially unsettling. In the United States, identity is often intertwined with activity. Busyness confers value. Achievement provides narrative coherence. Abroad, especially in cultures that prize balance over ambition, that scaffolding loosens. Days may feel quieter. Accomplishments less visible. Progress less quantifiable. The absence of constant striving can feel, at first, like a loss of purpose.

For many, this discomfort gives way to clarity. They begin to notice how much of their former life was reactive—responding to demands rather than choosing direction. Abroad, time opens. Choices slow. Meaning is no longer imposed externally; it must be articulated internally. This is not always easy, but it is profoundly generative. People begin to ask different questions: "How do I want to spend my attention? What kind of contribution feels authentic at this stage of my life? What does "enough" actually look like?"

Work, if it continues, often changes character. Some expatriates reduce hours, consult selectively, or pursue projects aligned with interest rather than necessity. Others retire entirely, discovering that meaning need not be tethered to income. Still others create new ventures—not out of ambition, but curiosity. Teaching, mentoring, writing, volunteering, and creative pursuits frequently take on greater importance. Contribution becomes less about scale and more about resonance.

This recalibration extends to material life as well. Many expatriates discover that abundance feels different abroad. Without constant exposure to advertising and consumption-driven environments, desires soften. Smaller homes feel sufficient. Fewer possessions feel freeing. Quality replaces quantity. The question shifts from "Can I afford this?" to "Do I need this?" and often, "Does this add anything to my life?"

The concept of "enough" becomes central. Enough space. Enough income. Enough activity. Enough connection. In cultures where moderation is normalized, enough is not a compromise but a value. Americans often arrive with deeply ingrained assumptions that more is always better—more space, more speed, more choice. Living abroad challenges this reflex. It reveals that satisfaction is not linearly correlated with accumulation.

Meaning also emerges through place itself. Landscapes, seasons, and public spaces shape daily experience in ways that are easy to overlook until they change. Access to nature, proximity to water, walkable neighborhoods, and shared civic spaces all contribute to a sense of well-being that feels embodied rather than conceptual. Life abroad often feels more spatially integrated. One does not drive past life to get to it; one moves through it.

Over time, expatriates frequently report a heightened sense of presence. Without the constant pull of distraction, they become more attentive—to weather, to conversation, to the passing of time. Days feel longer, not because more happens, but because attention is less fragmented. This presence is not dramatic. It is quiet and cumulative. It is felt in unhurried meals, familiar walks, and the pleasure of being known in small ways.

This does not mean life abroad is free of difficulty. Frustrations persist. Bureaucracy remains slow. Cultural misunderstandings still occur. Moments of homesickness arise unexpectedly. But these challenges are integrated into life rather than dominating it. They become part of the texture rather than obstacles to overcome. The emotional amplitude flattens. Extremes soften. Life becomes steadier.

The most significant transformation is how expatriates relate to success. Success abroad is rarely visible or performative. It does not announce itself through promotions or possessions. Instead, it reveals itself through equilibrium: waking up without dread, feeling physically well, having time for relationships, and a sense that one's days align with one's values.

This quiet success can be difficult to explain to those who remain embedded in more competitive environments. From the outside, expatriate life may appear modest, even diminished. From the inside, it often feels expansive. Not because it offers everything, but because it offers what matters.

As expatriates settle into this rhythm, many come to understand that living abroad was never about geography alone. It was about reclaiming authorship. About choosing how to live rather than inheriting a default. About recognizing that quality of life is not something granted by systems, but something assembled through daily choices, made consciously and repeatedly.

In this sense, expatriation becomes less an endpoint than a practice, an ongoing process of alignment between place and person, values and routines, intention and action. Some will remain abroad for decades. Others will return home changed by the experience. What endures is not the location, but the perspective.

Lifestyle design is not reserved for those who cross borders. It is simply more visible when they do. Living abroad strips life down to essentials and asks a question that resonates far beyond expatriation: If you could choose how your days unfold, what would you choose?

For many who live abroad, the answer is not grand. It is ordinary and deeply human. Time to walk. Time to talk. Time to eat well and rest well. Time to belong somewhere, imperfectly but genuinely. In a world that often demands urgency, this may be the most radical design choice of all.

Chapter 11

INTEGRATION, IDENTITY, & BELONGING

BECOMING AT HOME ABROAD

Part I: Between Arrival and Belonging

Psychologists sometimes describe a "third culture" experience—a condition in which identity is no longer anchored exclusively in a single national or cultural framework, but instead forms at the intersection of several. For some individuals, this hybridity feels liberating. Freed from the expectations of their home culture, they discover new ways of being—quieter, slower, less performative. For others, the ambiguity can feel unsettling, even lonely. Without clear social mirrors, they struggle to locate themselves. Often, both experiences coexist.

Charles's life illustrates this dynamic in a particularly layered way. He was born in Hawaii and is Caucasian in appearance, but he was raised in the local culture of Kīhei on the island of Maui. His childhood was immersed in everyday Hawaiian life, including local foods and the Pidgin language—a distinctive blend of English, Hawaiian, and street slang that functions as a cultural marker of belonging. His sense of identity was shaped less by formal ethnic or national categories than by place—by community rhythms, shared practices, and a lived sense of belonging that had little to do with what his passport declared as nationality. Hawaii felt like home not because of ancestry, but because it was experienced daily.

As an adult, Charles chose to move to Valletta, Malta, initially without a job or a clear professional plan. His father was Maltese, which meant Charles could legally reside in Malta. Yet legality did not translate into familiarity or comfort. Malta was familiar in theory, inherited through lineage, but unfamiliar in practice. In a sense, he was returning to something he had never actually inhabited.

Charles eventually settled in Malta and found employment in the financial sector. It was there that he met Emi, a Japanese national working in Malta's legal sector. Their relationship developed across cultural and geographic boundaries. After marrying, they eventually both became Maltese citizens, building a shared life in a country that was home to them both, yet native to neither. Emi, raised in Japan, and Charles, shaped by life in Hawaii, initially felt uncertain navigating Maltese culture. Over time, however, they came to appreciate the process of adaptation itself—the gradual learning of customs, rhythms, and social expectations that slowly transformed unfamiliar surroundings into something more comfortable.

From the outside, this progression might appear to represent resolution: ancestry reclaimed, citizenship secured, borders crossed with intention. In reality, the journey was anything but direct. Belonging did not arrive the moment a visa was granted or a passport issued. Instead, it emerged slowly and unevenly across years and places. Each move reshaped identity rather than completing it.

Charles and Emi's experience reflects a reality that many expatriates eventually discover: finding a sense of belonging is often circuitous. It does not follow legal logic and is rarely guaranteed by ancestry, documentation, or length of residence. One can be culturally fluent yet socially peripheral. One can be legally local yet emotionally foreign. And sometimes one feels most at home in places where, at first glance, it might appear one does not belong at all.

Expatriates frequently describe an initial sense of relief upon leaving the United States. The absence of familiar pressures can feel like stepping out of a storm. Daily life feels calmer, more humane. Yet over time, relief gives way to reflection. Distance reveals not only what one disliked about home, but what one unconsciously relied upon.

Cultural defaults are powerful precisely because they are invisible. They shape how people express emotion, how they relate to time, how they signal trust or respect. When those defaults no longer apply, everyday interactions require interpretation. A delayed response may signal indifference or politeness. Directness may be refreshing or rude. Silence may be comfortable or tense. Without shared assumptions, meaning becomes negotiable.

This constant negotiation can be exhausting. Even when things are going well, expatriates may feel a low-level cognitive load. The world requires more interpretation than it once did. Over time, this can produce a subtle form of fatigue that is not tied to workload but to vigilance.

At the same time, this heightened awareness can be profoundly illuminating. Removed from cultural autopilot, expatriates often see themselves more clearly. Habits once assumed to be personal reveal themselves as cultural. Preferences once defended as universal are exposed as contextual. The experience can be humbling, occasionally uncomfortable, and deeply clarifying.

Many Americans report that living abroad changes how "American" they feel. Some discover that they are more so than they realized—their communication style, expectations of service, and sense of time shaped by norms they never consciously chose. Others find that aspects of American identity fall away quickly, replaced by values they did not know they held until circumstances allowed them to emerge.

What complicates this process is that integration is often misunderstood. Many assume that to integrate is to assimilate—to lose one's distinctiveness to fit in. This fear leads some expatriates to keep emotional distance, maintaining a stance of permanent observer. Others swing too far in the opposite direction, attempting to erase their origins in pursuit of acceptance. Both approaches tend to fail.

True integration is neither disappearance nor dominance. It is participation with integrity. It involves learning local customs not as performances but as expressions of shared meaning. It requires engaging with community life even when it feels awkward or slow to develop. It demands respect without self-erasure, curiosity without entitlement. Integration is less about blending in than about showing up consistently, imperfectly, and with humility.

This distinction matters because belonging cannot be forced. It cannot be rushed, and it cannot be measured precisely. It is built through repetition and trust in ordinary acts—greeting neighbors, returning to the same café, participating in local rituals. Over time, these acts accumulate into recognition. You are no longer merely present; you are expected.

The emotional journey toward belonging is rarely linear. There are periods of confidence followed by unexpected waves of doubt. Holidays can be particularly difficult, as traditions feel displaced and time zones emphasize distance from loved ones. Illness or crisis may amplify feelings of vulnerability. In such moments, expatriates may question their choices, wondering whether the sense of dislocation is a sign that they do not truly belong anywhere.

Yet these moments are not failures. They are part of the long game of integration. Because becoming at home abroad is not about arriving somewhere new; it is about becoming someone new—without losing yourself along the way.

Part II: Learning to Participate

Many Americans arrive abroad fluent in logistics but hesitant about participation. They know how to comply with systems, but are less sure how to enter social life without intruding. This is understandable: cultural missteps feel more consequential when one is a guest. The fear of offending, of being misunderstood, or of confirming stereotypes can lead to a kind of polite withdrawal. Life becomes efficient but thin.

Participation begins with accepting that mistakes are inevitable—and survivable.

Every culture has unwritten rules, governing how people greet one another, how they express disagreement, how they signal trust or distance. They are rarely explained explicitly, because locals learn them by osmosis. For expatriates, these norms must be inferred through observation and error. The learning process can be humbling. It can also be profoundly connective.

Language is often the most visible barrier to participation, but it is also the most powerful bridge. Fluency matters less than effort. Even limited language ability changes the tone of interaction. It signals respect, curiosity, and willingness to meet others halfway. A halting sentence offered sincerely often invites warmth in a way perfect silence never does.

Many expatriates delay language learning until they feel "ready." In practice, language improves fastest when it is embedded in daily life—through routine conversations, shared activities, and repeated exposure. Participation accelerates learning, and learning deepens participation. The two are inseparable.

Community life provides another pathway into belonging. This does not require formal civic engagement or deep friendships immediately. It begins with proximity: frequenting the same places, attending local events, becoming a familiar face. Over time, recognition develops. Small exchanges turn into conversations. Conversations turn into relationships. The process is slow, but cumulative.

Americans accustomed to efficiency may find this pace frustrating, but integration abroad does not respond well to optimization. It cannot be scheduled or accelerated. It unfolds according to local rhythms, which may privilege trust over speed and continuity over novelty. Accepting this tempo is itself an act of integration.

Expatriates who struggle most with belonging are often those who remain observers rather than participants. They know a great deal about the culture, but interact little with it. They consume experiences rather than inhabit them. Over time, this distance becomes self-reinforcing. The place remains interesting but never intimate.

Participation also requires selective adaptation. Integration does not mean adopting every local custom uncritically. It means understanding the logic behind behaviors and choosing how to respond authentically. Some practices will resonate deeply. Others will not. Integration allows for discernment without dismissal.

This balance is especially important for Americans, whose cultural style often emphasizes directness, efficiency, and individual autonomy. In some contexts, these traits are appreciated. In others, they are perceived as abrupt or self-centered. Learning when to soften, when to slow down, and when to listen rather than explain is part of cultural literacy. It does not diminish one's identity; it refines it.

As participation deepens, many expatriates notice a shift in how they are perceived. They move from being "the American" to being a specific person—someone known for their habits, temperament, and presence rather than their nationality alone. This transition is subtle but meaningful: it signals that one has crossed from novelty into familiarity.

At the same time, integration can expose unexpected tensions. As expatriates adopt local habits, they may feel increasingly out of step with friends or family back home. Conversations can feel misaligned. Assumptions no longer match. This divergence can feel destabilizing or provoke guilt or confusion. The sense of belonging abroad may be accompanied by a sense of partial estrangement from home. This is not a betrayal of origin; it is a consequence of growth, a sign that the experience of expatriation is doing its deeper work of reshaping perspective.

Participation often unfolds unevenly within families. Children may integrate faster, particularly through school and play. They acquire language intuitively and absorb social norms with less self-consciousness. Parents, by contrast, may struggle longer, navigating adult social worlds with fewer entry points. This asymmetry can invert traditional roles, with children becoming cultural guides. When embraced rather than resisted, this reversal can strengthen family bonds and model adaptability.

Participation is not constant. There will be periods of withdrawal—times when energy dips or frustration rises. Integration allows for these pauses. Belonging is not undone by retreat, provided one returns. The danger lies not in stepping back, but in staying there indefinitely.

What distinguishes long-term expatriates from perpetual outsiders is not perfection, but persistence. They continue engaging even when it feels awkward. They accept partial belonging as sufficient. They allow relationships to form gradually rather than demanding immediate depth.

By the time participation becomes habitual, something important has shifted. The host culture no longer feels like a puzzle to be solved. It feels like a context to be lived within. The expatriate no longer asks constantly whether they belong. They act as though they do—and over time, that assumption becomes true.

Part III: Becoming Without Losing

One of the most persistent myths surrounding expatriation is that it requires choosing between identities. Am I still American, or have I become something else? This binary framing creates unnecessary tension. Identity does not operate on a zero-sum basis. It layers. It accumulates. It adapts to context without dissolving into contradiction. This question of identity is not about nationality alone. It is about coherence, how to hold the person one has been with the person one is becoming.

For many Americans, identity at home is reinforced constantly and unconsciously. Shared references, cultural shorthand, and national narratives provide a backdrop against which individuality can stand out. Living abroad, that backdrop disappears, revealing how much of identity is contextual rather than intrinsic. Habits once considered personal are revealed as cultural defaults; preferences once defended as universal are exposed as contingent. This unraveling can be disorienting, but it also creates space for choice.

Expatriates often describe a process of selective reintegration—deciding consciously which parts of their former identity to carry forward and which to release. This is an act of authorship. Living abroad invites people to edit themselves, not to erase their past but to refine it.

Many long-term expatriates come to understand identity as situational rather than singular. They feel American in certain settings and deeply aligned with their host culture in others. They may be critical of aspects of the United States while remaining emotionally attached to it. They may adopt local customs without claiming full insider status. This fluidity is not confusion; it is competence.

Belonging, in this sense, is not about total integration or cultural purity. It is about legitimacy—the sense that one's presence is appropriate and recognized. Legitimacy arises through participation, consistency, and care. It is felt when one's absence would be noticed, when one's voice carries weight in small ways, when one is included not out of politeness but expectation.

Home, too, undergoes redefinition. For expatriates, home is rarely a single place after being abroad long enough. It becomes relational rather than geographic, residing in routines, relationships, and internal states rather than coordinates. This multiplicity can feel unsettling at first, particularly in cultures that emphasize rootedness and permanence. Over time, it often feels expansive.

Returning "home" to the United States can sharpen this awareness. Familiar places may feel strangely distant. Cultural intensity may feel overwhelming. Conversations may move at a different speed. This reverse culture shock can be more disorienting than the initial move abroad. It highlights how deeply expatriation has reshaped perception.

Yet this distance does not negate belonging. It reveals transformation. Expatriates often find that they no longer fit neatly into a single narrative, and that is precisely the point. They have learned to live between frameworks rather than within a single one. They are comfortable with ambiguity. They recognize that identity is not fixed, but responsive.

For families, this layered identity becomes intergenerational. Children raised abroad often develop a natural fluency in cultural code-switching, moving between languages, norms, and expectations with ease. This adaptability can be a source of strength, but it also requires support. Children need permission to claim all parts of their identity without pressure to resolve them into a single answer.

Parents who model this acceptance help children internalize complexity as a feature rather than a flaw.

There are moments, of course, when the weight of in-betweenness feels heavy. Illness, loss, or crisis can amplify feelings of distance from extended family or familiar systems. In such moments, expatriates may long for the simplicity of a singular home. These feelings do not invalidate the choice to live abroad. They remind us that belonging is emotional as much as it is practical.

What sustains expatriates through these moments is not certainty, but commitment. Commitment to place, even when it frustrates. Commitment to relationships, even when they develop slowly. Commitment to self-understanding, even when it reveals contradictions. Integration is not about eliminating tension; it is about learning to live within it without becoming fractured by it.

In time, many expatriates stop asking whether they belong. The question loses urgency. Belonging becomes something they enact rather than evaluate. They participate without self-consciousness. They contribute without overthinking their role. The place they once studied now simply holds them. This is not assimilation, nor is it detachment. It is maturity.

Becoming at home abroad does not mean arriving at a final identity. It means accepting identity as ongoing. It means recognizing that who you are is shaped by where you live, but not confined to it. It means understanding that integration is not something you complete, but something you practice.

In the broader arc of this book, this chapter marks a turning point. Initially, we focused on movement—why people leave, how they relocate, and how they design lives across borders. Here, we turn inward, asking what all that movement does to the self. I believe the answer is not loss, but expansion.

Expatriation does not require abandoning one's past. It requires holding it differently. It invites people to become more aware of who they are when stripped of defaults, and more deliberate about who they choose to be in response.

Belonging, in the end, is not a destination. It is a relationship—between person and place, between memory and possibility. Those who learn to cultivate it abroad often carry that skill wherever they go. They become at home not because the world conforms to them, but because they have learned how to meet the world with presence, humility, and care.

In a time of accelerating change, this may be the deepest lesson expatriation offers: that home is not something we find once and keep forever. It is something we learn how to build—again and again—without losing ourselves in the process.

Chapter 12

COMMUNITY, CITIZENSHIP, & GIVING BACK

BECOMING PART OF A PLACE

Part I: From Guest to Neighbor

Every expatriate arrives as a guest.

At first, this status is both obvious and appropriate. You are learning the rules, the language, the rhythms of daily life. You are absorbing rather than contributing, focused inward on survival and adjustment. You ask practical questions: how things work, where to go, what to avoid. Your energy is consumed by the mechanics of settling in, as it should be. Before you can give, you must first understand.

But something changes if you stay.

Over time, the novelty wears off. You stop noticing every difference. You begin to anticipate patterns rather than react to them. You develop routines that no longer feel provisional. With that shift comes a quiet, often unspoken pull: the sense that living somewhere is no longer just about what the place offers you, but about what you owe in return.

This is the moment expatriation deepens.

It is easy to imagine life abroad as a transaction. Lower costs in exchange for distance. Better weather in exchange for inconvenience. Calm in exchange for familiarity. Many people approach expatriation this way, consciously or not. They optimize for lifestyle and stop there. For some, this is enough. But for many others, something begins to feel thin if the relationship remains one-sided. Belonging does not grow through consumption.

At a certain point, expatriates who remain psychologically invested in a place start to ask different questions. They notice local challenges rather than just local charms. They care what happens to the neighborhood, the school, the market, the landscape. They feel affected when things go wrong, and proud when things go well. The place begins to matter not just instrumentally, but emotionally.

This is the shift from guest to neighbor.

Being a neighbor is not about legal status or length of residence. It is about orientation. A guest observes; a neighbor participates. A guest asks what is allowed; a neighbor asks what is needed. The difference is subtle, but profound. It marks the point at which expatriation stops being primarily about authorship and starts to include responsibility.

The path from guest to neighbor is informal and deeply contextual. There is no formal initiation into community life for newcomers, especially foreigners. It unfolds through presence, curiosity, and repeated small acts rather than declarations of intent.

Often, it begins with attention. Paying attention to local events rather than just national headlines. Learning the history of the place, not as trivia, but as context for how people think and behave. Noticing what is valued, what is contested, and what is quietly endured. Attention is the foundation of care. Without it, engagement risks becoming superficial or intrusive.

From attention grows participation. Attending festivals not as a tourist, but as a participant. Supporting local businesses not out of novelty, but loyalty. Showing up consistently enough to be recognized, to be missed when absent. These acts may seem modest, but they signal commitment. They say: I am not merely passing through.

For many expatriates, this is where the expat bubble becomes visible—and uncomfortable. Expat communities provide comfort and familiarity, especially in the early stages of relocation. Staying entirely within an expat bubble is not morally wrong. It is understandable, and in some cases necessary. They offer shared language, shared frustrations, and shared shortcuts. But if these communities are the sole locus of social life, they can also be barriers to deeper integration.

Moving beyond the bubble does not require abandoning expat friendships. It requires expanding the circle. It means allowing local relationships to develop even when they are slower, less immediately rewarding, and occasionally uncomfortable. It means accepting that you may always be "from somewhere else," but that this does not disqualify you from participation.

In fact, in many communities, outsiders who show genuine interest and respect are welcomed precisely because they bring different perspectives without a sense of entitlement. The key is humility. Offering help rather than solutions. Listening before speaking. Recognizing that good intentions do not excuse cultural insensitivity.

One of the most powerful ways expatriates become neighbors is by helping other newcomers. This role emerges naturally once you have navigated the systems yourself: you remember the confusion, the anxiety, the small victories. Sharing that knowledge—pointing someone toward a resource, explaining a process, offering reassurance—creates a sense of continuity. It positions you not just as a beneficiary of the place, but as a contributor to its social fabric.

Over time, you are no longer merely present; you are embedded. People begin to ask your opinion because you are involved. You are trusted not because you are local, but because you are consistent.

There is no single moment when the transition from guest to neighbor is complete. Instead, it is felt gradually, in subtle shifts of perception. The place stops feeling like somewhere you are allowed to be and starts feeling like somewhere you belong—conditionally, imperfectly, but genuinely. With belonging comes responsibility.

This does not mean taking over or imposing one's values, but recognizing that your actions have impact and that your choices—where you spend money, how you speak, what you support—shape the community you live in. It means understanding that even as a foreigner, you are part of the ecosystem.

This realization sets the stage for deeper questions about residency, citizenship, and civic life. What does it mean to commit to a place legally, not just emotionally? What rights and obligations come with long-term residence? And how do expatriates navigate the line between participation and overreach?

Part II: Planting Roots — Residency, Citizenship, and Civic Life

Once expatriates begin to feel like neighbors rather than guests, a new set of questions emerges—not just about belonging, but about commitment. Emotional attachment to a place often precedes legal attachment, but over time, the gap between the two can feel uncomfortable. You may love where you live, contribute to its daily life, and plan to stay indefinitely, yet still exist on a temporary legal footing. This tension invites reflection on what it means to plant roots in a place that was once only a destination.

Long-stay visas, digital nomad permits, retirement visas, or extended tourist arrangements provide a foothold, but not a foundation. They allow time to experiment, to test compatibility, to decide whether the move is sustainable. This provisional phase is essential. It protects against premature commitment and acknowledges that belonging cannot be rushed.

But if a life abroad endures, temporary status begins to feel increasingly fragile. Renewals loom. Rules change. Bureaucratic uncertainty becomes a recurring stressor. What once felt adventurous can begin to feel precarious. It is at this point that many expatriates start to explore longer-term residency—not just as a legal upgrade, but as a signal of intention.

Residency is more than paperwork. It is a declaration that you plan to stay, to invest time and energy in a place beyond a fixed horizon. It often comes with tangible benefits: greater stability, easier renewals, access to public services, and protection from sudden policy shifts. Just as importantly, it carries symbolic weight, marking a transition from provisional presence to recognized participation.

The process of securing long-term residency can be sobering. It requires patience, documentation, and often years of compliance. Income thresholds must be met. Health coverage maintained. Absences tracked. Language requirements fulfilled. The path is rarely linear, and it varies widely by country. Yet for many expatriates, the effort itself becomes part of the integration process. It demands engagement with institutions, familiarity with laws, and respect for local rules—an education in how the society organizes itself.

Permanent residency, where available, deepens this relationship further. It reduces administrative friction and offers a sense of security that temporary status cannot. You are less vulnerable to policy changes, more confident in long-term planning, and often better integrated into public systems. While permanent residency does not erase foreignness, it acknowledges permanence. It says, "You are expected to be here."

For some expatriates, residency is enough. It provides stability without requiring a redefinition of national identity. Others, however, feel drawn toward an even deeper form of commitment: citizenship.

The motivations for pursuing citizenship vary. Some seek freedom of movement, especially in regions where citizenship opens borders otherwise closed. Others view it as a hedge against political or economic instability. Still others pursue it for family reasons, wanting to pass options to their children or formalize ties built over many years. For a few, citizenship represents gratitude—a way of affirming commitment to a society that has offered opportunity and refuge.

Yet citizenship also raises difficult questions. It is not merely a status; it is a set of obligations. Taxes, civic duties, and legal responsibilities may follow. Dual citizenship, while permitted by the United States, is not universally accepted.

Second citizenship is a topic of growing interest among Americans living abroad, not only as a practical asset but as an existential one. Holding citizenship in another country reshapes how one understands belonging. It formalizes what may already feel true emotionally—that this place is not just where you live, but part of who you are.

Some countries require renunciation of prior nationality, forcing a choice that is as emotional as it is legal. The decision to naturalize should never be made lightly. It asks not only where you live, but where you stand.

Even without local citizenship, expatriates remain citizens of the United States. This fact carries its own responsibilities, particularly political ones. Living abroad does not sever civic ties to one's home country. Americans retain the right to vote and, with it, a voice in decisions that shape domestic and foreign policy alike. Distance can dull engagement, but it does not eliminate consequence. Policies enacted at home ripple outward, affecting immigration rules, taxation, diplomacy, and global stability.

Many expatriates find that living abroad sharpens their political awareness rather than diminishing it. Seeing the United States from the outside provides perspective. It reveals which systems are exceptional and which are simply different. It highlights assumptions once taken for granted. This vantage point can deepen civic responsibility, making participation feel more considered rather than reflexive.

At the same time, expatriates must navigate political engagement in their host countries with care. Even where voting rights are extended to non-citizens at local levels, participation requires cultural literacy and restraint. Advocacy without understanding can quickly become overreach. The most effective engagement often begins not with policy positions, but with listening, learning how issues are framed locally, who is affected, and why debates unfold as they do.

Civic life abroad is less about assertion and more about alignment. It asks expatriates to recognize that participation is a privilege, not an entitlement. That legitimacy grows from contribution rather than critique. And that responsibility increases with duration of stay.

What emerges is a more nuanced understanding of citizenship itself. Citizenship is often imagined as a binary—one either has it or does not. In practice, it operates along a spectrum. There is legal citizenship, defined by passports and rights. There is civic citizenship, expressed through participation and contribution. And there is moral citizenship, reflected in how one treats the place and people among whom one lives.

Expatriates occupy a complex position within this spectrum. They may lack formal citizenship while exercising meaningful civic presence. They may hold multiple legal identities while feeling emotionally anchored in more than one place. Rather than resolving these tensions, many learn to live within them, recognizing that belonging does not require exclusivity.

Planting roots abroad is not about replacing one allegiance with another. It is about expanding the circle of responsibility, acknowledging that if you benefit from a place, you owe it care. If you plan to stay, you must contribute. And if you seek belonging, you must be willing to share in both the privileges and the burdens of community life.

Part III: Contribution, Care, and the Ethics of Belonging

If residency and citizenship represent formal commitments to a place, contribution represents an ethical one. It is here—beyond visas and paperwork—that expatriate life reaches its deepest expression. To contribute is not merely to help: it is to recognize oneself as part of an ecosystem, bound by mutual dependence and shared consequence. It is to move from presence to care.

For many expatriates, the impulse to give back arises naturally once life stabilizes. Survival no longer consumes all available energy. Routines settle. Relationships form. The place begins to feel familiar enough to notice its needs as clearly as its pleasures. What once appeared charming now reveals complexity. What once felt idyllic now shows strain. This awareness is not disillusionment; it is intimacy.

Foreigners often arrive with resources—financial, educational, or experiential—that exceed those of many locals. This imbalance creates both opportunity and risk. When expatriates give without understanding, they may inadvertently reinforce hierarchies or disrupt fragile systems. When they offer solutions without listening, they may replicate the very dynamics they sought to leave behind. Ideally, contribution begins with humility. The most meaningful contributions start not with action, but with observation.

Listening to local voices. Learning how problems are already being addressed. Understanding what input is welcomed and what is sensitive. Recognizing that help is not always needed, and that presence itself can be a form of support. In many cases, expatriates discover that the most valuable contribution is not money or expertise, but reliability—showing up consistently, respecting local leadership, and committing to the long term.

Volunteering is often the most visible pathway into contribution, but it is not the only one. Teaching language skills, mentoring young people, supporting schools or health initiatives, and participating in environmental stewardship are ways to engage. Actions do not need to be grand to be meaningful. In fact, small-scale, sustained involvement often has greater impact than episodic gestures.

Giving back also reshapes the expatriate's internal landscape. It grounds life abroad in reciprocity rather than consumption. It shifts focus outward, reducing the isolation that can accompany relocation. Studies consistently show that people who volunteer experience greater well-being, stronger social ties, and a deeper sense of purpose. For expatriates, these benefits are magnified as contribution becomes a bridge between worlds, anchoring identity in service rather than status.

There is also a quieter form of contribution that often goes unnoticed: economic participation. Supporting local businesses, artisans, farmers, and service providers keeps money circulating within the community. Choosing long-term rentals over short-term speculation can stabilize neighborhoods. Ethical consumption, while imperfect, signals respect for local livelihoods. These choices, repeated daily, shape the fabric of place as surely as formal volunteering.

Environmental stewardship is another domain where expatriates can contribute meaningfully. Many are drawn abroad by landscapes—coasts, mountains, forests—that are threatened by overdevelopment or climate change. Living in these places confers responsibility. Reducing waste, respecting local ecosystems, supporting conservation efforts, and advocating for sustainable practices where appropriate all reflect an ethic of care that extends beyond personal enjoyment.

Advocacy also has its place, though it demands caution. Expatriates occupy a delicate position when engaging with social or political issues in their host countries. Speaking out without understanding context can alienate allies or inflame tensions. Yet silence in the face of injustice can feel complicit. Navigating this terrain requires humility, patience, and a willingness to follow rather than lead. Often, the most ethical stance is to support local movements quietly rather than positioning oneself at the forefront.

Over time, expatriates who contribute thoughtfully find that their relationship to the place changes. They are no longer merely beneficiaries of its advantages. They share in its struggles. They feel pride in its successes and sorrow in its losses. The place becomes not just where they live, but something they care about deeply.

This transformation also reframes the idea of global citizenship. In an era defined by climate change, migration, and interconnected crises, borders no longer contain consequences. Expatriates, by virtue of their mobility, inhabit this reality acutely. They experience firsthand how systems intersect—how policies in one country affect lives in another, how economic choices ripple across regions, how environmental degradation respects no passport.

Being a global citizen, in this sense, is not about abstraction, but about responsibility at scale. It is about recognizing that mobility confers both privilege and obligation, that the ability to move, to choose where one lives, carries with it a duty to act with care wherever one lands.

This does not require perfection. No expatriate fully escapes the asymmetries of power embedded in global systems. What it does require is awareness and intention. A willingness to ask not only how to optimize one's life, but how to align it ethically. A readiness to give back in proportion to what one receives.

There are pitfalls along this path. Isolation can masquerade as self-sufficiency. Overconfidence can masquerade as leadership. Detachment can masquerade as neutrality. Avoiding these traps requires ongoing reflection and remembering that belonging is not a static achievement, but a practice renewed through action.

For many expatriates, this realization marks the final evolution of life abroad. The journey begins with escape or curiosity, moves through adaptation and integration, and matures into contribution. The expatriate is no longer simply someone who lives elsewhere, but someone who participates—who helps shape the place, even in small ways, through daily choices and sustained care.

In a world increasingly shaped by displacement and change, the line between expatriate and migrant, visitor and resident, grows porous. To live in a new climate—environmental, political, or cultural—is not merely to seek refuge; it is to accept relationship.

What distinguishes a life lived responsibly abroad is not duration or status, but engagement. Survival and flourishing are collective endeavors, shaped by how we show up for one another. You do not need to solve the world's problems to belong. You do not need to erase your origins or adopt a new identity wholesale. You need only recognize that where you live, you matter—and that how you live there matters too.

That, ultimately, is what it means to become part of a place—not by claiming it, but by caring for it alongside those who call it home.

Chapter 13

THE EMOTIONAL ARC OF EXPATRIATION

GRIEF, GROWTH, AND COMING FULL CIRCLE

Part I: The Unseen Cost of a New Life

By the time someone reaches this point in the journey to a life abroad, it is tempting to believe the hardest work is behind them. Visas were secured, logistics resolved, language learned well enough to function. Routines are established. On the surface, life works. In many cases, it works better than it ever did before.

And yet, beneath that stability, something quieter begins to make itself known.

Expatriation, no matter how intentional or well-considered, carries loss. Not dramatic or even visible loss, but slow, accumulative loss—the kind that reveals itself in moments you did not anticipate and emotions you did not expect to feel. Even when the move was chosen freely, even when it delivered everything it promised, something was left behind. This is the unseen cost of a new life.

Most people expect homesickness in the early days. They brace for it. What surprises them is how grief reappears later, once the novelty fades and the adrenaline subsides. It surfaces not exactly as longing for the old life, but as a sense of dislocation, a quiet awareness that some things can never be fully carried forward.

It might arrive in the form of food that tastes almost right, but not quite. A holiday that passes without ceremony. A familiar joke that no longer lands because the cultural shorthand is gone. Or a moment of guilt when you realize you missed something important back home, and no amount of explanation will make that absence feel acceptable.

This grief is often minimized, especially by those who chose to leave voluntarily. After all, you wanted this. You planned for it. You knew what you were giving up. And yet, that knowledge does not eliminate feeling. Grief does not require regret; it only requires attachment.

Expat grief is subtle because it coexists with gratitude. You can love your new life and mourn your old one at the same time. You can feel relieved to be gone and ache for what you left behind. These contradictions deepen the experience. But because they resist simple narratives, many expats struggle to name them. They carry grief quietly, unsure whether it is legitimate. It is.

Leaving a country is not only a geographic departure. It is a psychological one. You leave behind not just people and places, but versions of yourself—roles you once played effortlessly, identities that were affirmed without question. Professional status, cultural fluency, and social ease often dissolve overnight. Abroad, you may be respected, welcomed, even admired—but rarely in the same way you were before.

This loss can feel particularly sharp for those whose identity was closely tied to career or social standing. Abroad, credentials may not translate. Titles may not matter. Accomplishments may require explanation. In some contexts, they may not matter at all. You are reduced, in the best and worst sense, to who you are rather than what you've done. Some find this liberating. Others find it disorienting. Most experience both.

There is also the grief of distance, from family milestones, from aging parents, from the quiet accumulation of shared memory that happens only when lives overlap consistently. Video calls soften the edge but do not erase it. You are present, but not embodied. Involved, but not fully woven in. Over time, this partial presence can feel heavy, especially during moments of loss or celebration.

Another layer of grief emerges when you realize that the place you left behind continues to change without you. The United States you remember slowly becomes historical rather than current. Cultural references shift. Political landscapes evolve. Even familiar neighborhoods transform. When you return, if you return, you may find yourself disoriented—not because the place has changed, but because you have.

This realization carries its own mourning. You cannot go back to what was, because it no longer exists. And neither do you, in the same way.

Many expatriates struggle most during this phase because it lacks clear resolution. There is no single object of grief, no defined moment of loss. Instead, it is a series of small recognitions that accumulate over time. A sense that something essential has moved out of reach—not because you failed to hold onto it, but because life has carried you somewhere else.

Grief is not an error in the expatriate journey. It is evidence that the journey mattered.

Only meaningful change produces meaningful loss. Only attachment creates mourning. The presence of grief does not suggest that expatriation was a mistake. It suggests that it was transformative.

What makes this phase particularly complex is that grief often arrives alongside growth. At the same time you are learning new ways of being, expanding your worldview, and building a life that feels more aligned with your values, you are also shedding identities and comforts that once defined you. The psyche must hold both processes at once. This is emotionally demanding work.

Many expatriates attempt to outrun this discomfort. They stay busy. They travel constantly. They distract themselves with logistics or novelty. Others turn inward too sharply, withdrawing from connection. Neither extreme resolves grief. It only postpones it. The healthier path lies in acknowledgment.

Naming loss allows it to integrate rather than fester. It allows grief to coexist with gratitude without demanding resolution. It allows expatriates to stop judging themselves for feelings that do not fit a tidy narrative of success or escape.

Grief, when honored, becomes a teacher. It clarifies what mattered. It sharpens values. It deepens empathy—for others who have left, for migrants who had no choice, for family members who stayed behind. It widens the emotional lens through which expatriates see the world.

This is why expatriation is not simply a lifestyle decision. It is a psychological crossing.

And like all crossings, it demands something of you.

Part II: The Middle Space — Living Between Worlds

After the initial grief has been acknowledged—if not resolved—many expatriates enter what might be called the middle space. Not a place on any map, it is a very real psychological territory. Here, the sharp edges of transition soften, yet full belonging has not quite settled in. Life is functional, sometimes even joyful, but also strangely unmoored. You are no longer who you were before, and not entirely sure who you are becoming.

This is the phase that most clearly defies simple explanation.

In the middle space, expatriates often feel suspended between identities. In the host country, you may still be marked as foreign. At the same time, when you return to the United States or speak with friends back home, you may feel unexpectedly out of step. This in-betweenness can feel isolating. Humans are wired for belonging, and belonging traditionally implies a clear inside and outside. Expat life disrupts that binary. You are both insider and outsider, everywhere and nowhere at once.

The middle space is where expatriates begin to confront the limits of identity as something fixed. For some, this ambiguity feels destabilizing. For others, it becomes a source of insight. When cultural belonging is no longer guaranteed by geography, identity must be reconstructed more consciously. Values come to the forefront. What do I actually care about? What rhythms support me? What do I want to organize my life around?

These questions often arise not in moments of crisis, but in daily contrasts that accumulate into reflection. Standing in line at a government office. Watching children navigate school in another language. Observing how conflict is handled differently, how time is valued differently, and how success is defined differently.

Many expatriates describe this phase as one of deep introspection. Without the familiar signals that once affirmed who they were, they are forced to listen inward. External noise recedes. The internal compass becomes louder. This can be uncomfortable, particularly for those accustomed to external validation. But it is also where growth accelerates.

You can admire the efficiency of one system while valuing the humanity of another. You can critique aspects of American life while still loving the country deeply. You can feel gratitude for your adopted home while acknowledging that it is not perfect. This cognitive flexibility is not indecision. It is maturity. Expatriates who remain open often develop a both/and worldview rather than an either/or one. They learn to hold contradictions without needing to resolve them immediately.

Emotionally, the middle space is often marked by oscillation. Periods of contentment followed by waves of doubt. Moments of belonging interrupted by sudden longing. These shifts can feel disconcerting, particularly when there is no clear cause. Many expatriates worry that this emotional variability signals instability or dissatisfaction. In reality, it signals integration in progress.

Belonging is not a linear ascent. It expands and contracts as circumstances change. A familiar holiday may trigger nostalgia. A new friendship may deepen attachment. A bureaucratic frustration may reignite the desire to leave. None of these moments define the journey on their own. Together, they shape it.

One of the quiet gifts of the middle space is a refined sense of values. Expatriates often find that living abroad clarifies what matters by stripping away what does not. This clarity can feel empowering. Many report a growing sense of agency—the feeling that they are actively authoring their lives rather than reacting to inherited scripts. They become more deliberate about how they spend energy, whom they invest in, and what they tolerate. This agency is not loud or performative but quiet and grounded.

At the same time, the middle space can be emotionally taxing. Without a singular place to call home, expatriates may feel a diffuse sense of rootlessness. They belong partially in many places, but fully in none. This can be especially pronounced during transitions—moving within the host country, changing jobs, or navigating family milestones from afar.

What helps in this phase is normalization. Understanding that the middle space is not a failure of integration, but a natural stage of transformation, similar to adolescence—an in-between state where identity is forming but not yet settled. Like adolescence, it can feel awkward, intense, and uncertain; like adolescence, it is temporary, even if its lessons endure.

Some expatriates try to escape the middle space by making drastic decisions—moving again, returning home prematurely, or committing to permanence before they feel ready. While these choices may be right for some, they are often driven by discomfort rather than clarity. Sitting with ambiguity, though challenging, allows deeper integration to unfold organically.

Others learn to embrace the middle space as a feature rather than a flaw. They recognize that living between worlds affords a unique vantage point. It allows them to see assumptions from the outside, to question norms without rejecting them wholesale, and to empathize across cultural divides. This perspective can be profoundly enriching, even if it never resolves into a single sense of home.

Over time, the intensity of the middle space softens. The oscillation stabilizes. The expatriate becomes less preoccupied with where they belong and more engaged with how they live. Identity settles into something less brittle, more expansive. The question shifts from "Where is home?" to "What makes me feel at home?"

This shift marks the beginning of the final phase of the expatriate emotional arc—coming full circle. Not by returning to where one started, but by arriving at a deeper understanding of self, belonging, and choice.

Part III: Home Reimagined — Carrying the Circle Forward

At some point, expatriates realize that the questions that once preoccupied them have changed from early logistics (Can I do this? Where will I live? How will I manage?) to emotions (Do I belong? Have I lost something essential? Who am I becoming?). Now the question softens into something more reflective and less urgent: What does home mean to me now? This is the moment of coming full circle.

The moment is not marked by a decision to stay or leave, nor by a clear resolution of identity. It is marked by acceptance. Acceptance that life abroad has changed you, and that this change does not require justification. Acceptance that belonging is no longer singular or fixed. Acceptance that grief and gratitude can coexist.

For many, this realization arrives unexpectedly. It may come during a visit back to the United States, when familiar places feel oddly foreign. The pace feels faster, the noise louder, the assumptions more rigid. You recognize the culture intimately, yet you no longer move within it effortlessly. You are not alienated, exactly—but you are not fully at ease.

This experience, often called reverse culture shock, can be more disorienting than the original move abroad. At least abroad, you expected difference. At home, you expected familiarity. When that familiarity fails to materialize, the sense of displacement can feel profound.

Returning expatriates often report a loss of patience for things they once tolerated—bureaucracy, inefficiency, cultural aggression, the constant monetization of time. They may feel strangely invisible, as if their experiences abroad do not fit easily into the narratives others expect. Friends may listen politely but fail to grasp the depth of transformation. The expatriate realizes that while they left physically, they also returned psychologically changed.

This does not mean return is a mistake. It means return is not reversal.

Going back is not undoing. It is another stage of becoming. The person who returns carries different sensibilities, different thresholds, different values. Reintegration takes time. It may involve renegotiating relationships, redefining work, and recalibrating expectations. Some expatriates find this process invigorating, bringing global perspective into familiar spaces. Others find it constraining and eventually choose to leave again. There is no correct outcome.

Some expatriates remain abroad for the rest of their lives, building deep roots in their adopted countries. Some return permanently, enriched by what they gained and more deliberate about how they live at home. Others move again, following opportunity, family, or curiosity. Many live between worlds, maintaining multiple bases and fluid identities. The arc does not end in one place; it continues wherever life leads.

What unites these diverse endings is integration. The expatriate who has come full circle is no longer trying to resolve their experience into a single narrative of success or failure. They understand that expatriation was not about escape or reinvention alone. It was about engagement—with uncertainty, with difference, with self.

Home, at this stage, becomes less geographic and more relational. It may be a person, a set of routines, a language learned slowly and imperfectly. It may be a morning walk through a neighborhood that once felt alien and now feels intimate. It may be a kitchen that smells like blended cultures, or a community that knows you not as a foreigner first, but as yourself.

Home is felt rather than defined.

This reimagined sense of home carries forward even if circumstances change. Expatriates often discover that once they have lived deeply elsewhere, they are never quite the same anywhere. They have learned that belonging is constructed, not given. That comfort can be rebuilt. That identity can expand without shattering. These lessons travel with them.

Perhaps the most enduring gift of expatriation is the quiet confidence of adaptability. The knowledge that you can rebuild a life. That you can navigate unfamiliar systems, learn new languages, form new relationships. That you can sit with grief without being undone by it, and welcome change without needing to control it.

This confidence alters how expatriates move through the world. They become more empathetic toward others who are displaced or in transition. More patient with ambiguity. More intentional in their choices. They understand that life is not a linear progression toward a fixed ideal, but an ongoing negotiation between desire, circumstance, and values.

Looking back, many expatriates realize that while they left for practical reasons—climate, cost, politics, opportunity—what they found was something deeper. They found themselves in relief, seen against a different backdrop. They found values clarified by contrast. They found meaning in the act of choosing rather than inheriting.

This is why expatriation is never just about where you live. It is about how you relate to change. How you respond when the ground shifts beneath you. Whether you cling to certainty or cultivate resilience. Whether you narrow your world or expand it.

To live in a new climate—environmental, cultural, emotional—is to accept that life will ask more of you than comfort alone. It will ask for flexibility, humility, and courage. In return, it offers depth, perspective, and the rare chance to become more fully yourself through engagement with the unfamiliar.

You may have crossed borders. You may have changed languages. You may have lost and gained more than you anticipated. But if you have allowed the journey to shape you, then you have already arrived at something meaningful.

You did not just relocate. You redefined what it means to live.

Conclusion: Choosing How to Live in a Changing World

This book began with a question that once felt radical and now feels increasingly ordinary: Should I stay, should I leave, or can I do both? Along the way, that question stopped being only about geography and became a deeper inquiry into agency, belonging, and how to live well amid uncertainty.

If there is one truth that emerges, it is this: expatriation is not fundamentally about crossing borders. It is about crossing assumptions.

Many Americans begin this journey believing that place determines life—that opportunity, safety, affordability, or meaning are fixed attributes of a country rather than variables shaped by choices. Living abroad disrupts that belief. It reveals that much of what we accept as inevitable is, in fact, contingent. Systems can be different. Rhythms can be slower. Priorities can shift. Identity can expand.

Yet mobility should not be romanticized. Living abroad is not a cure for dissatisfaction, nor a guarantee of happiness. It introduces new challenges even as it resolves others. Bureaucracy replaces familiarity. Distance replaces proximity. Belonging must be built rather than assumed. Grief travels with you, even into the most beautiful places.

And still—despite the complexity, the ambiguity, and the emotional cost—many people who take this path would not trade it. Not because life abroad is perfect, but because it is intentional. It forces choice where inertia once ruled. It demands engagement where default once sufficed. It invites you to design your life rather than inherit it.

Throughout this book, we have explored expatriation from multiple angles: work and mobility, retirement and reinvention, emigration and legality, healthcare, education, family life, lifestyle design, identity, community, and emotional transformation. Taken together, these chapters form not a prescription, but a framework, a way of thinking clearly about life in a world that is changing faster than many of the institutions meant to support it.

For me, that framework has taken a very literal shape. I have sailed a good part of the world, long enough to know that movement does not have to mean restlessness. A modest-sized sailboat, I own, based in Malta-now feels less like an escape and more like a way of living deliberately. A place to stay, a place to move, a way to experience the Mediterranean while life remains in motion. Presently, it means continuing the Schengen Shuffle. Later, it may mean planting roots more firmly. The boat is not an alternative to home, but a way of negotiating what home can be. That, in many ways, is the point.

You may finish this book convinced that your future lies abroad. You may decide that staying where you are—armed with a new perspective—is the better choice. Or you may realize that the most resilient path lies somewhere in between, allowing your life to stretch across borders without being confined by them. All of these conclusions are valid.

What matters is not the outcome, but the posture.

To live in this new climate—environmental, political, economic, and emotional—requires adaptability. It requires humility about what we know and courage to act despite what we don't. It requires recognizing that stability is no longer guaranteed by staying put and that movement, when chosen consciously, can be a form of resilience rather than escape.

Home is not something you find once and keep forever. It is something you build—through relationships, routines, contribution, and care. Sometimes you build it where you were born. Sometimes you build it somewhere unexpected. Often, you build it more than once.

In a world defined by movement, climate change, and overlapping crises, the ability to rebuild—to adapt without losing yourself—may be one of the most important skills you can develop.

Wherever you live next, may you live with intention.

May you choose presence over fear, engagement over withdrawal, and curiosity over certainty.

And may you remember that the most important journey is not the one that takes you across borders, but the one that brings you closer to the life you actually want to live.

That choice—how to live—is yours.

Appendix:

Ten Countries, Real Examples, & How to Read the Rules

This book has focused on the why and the how of living abroad—the motivations, the emotional journey, the lifestyle shifts, and the deeper questions of belonging. This appendix shifts the lens toward something more concrete: entry requirements.

If there is one universal truth about relocating internationally, it is this: you do not simply arrive and stay. You are invited in—conditionally, temporarily, and according to rules that were written for the state's needs, not your convenience. Those rules matter. They shape who can enter, for how long, under what conditions, and with what obligations. They are also constantly evolving.

This appendix is not an exhaustive survey of every country or every visa pathway. Instead, it looks at ten countries I believe are particularly compelling options for Americans today, based on quality of life, accessibility, stability, and long-term viability. These countries are examples, not endorsements—and certainly not guarantees. They represent a cross-section of regions and bureaucratic styles that illustrate how different systems think about welcoming foreigners.

The information presented here draws in part from Global Citizen Solutions, a firm that tracks residency and citizenship pathways worldwide and publishes regularly updated guidance. At the time of writing, their summaries reflect current policy. But immigration law is not static. Thresholds change. Programs open and close. Requirements tighten or loosen in response to political, economic, or demographic pressures.

So read this appendix in the spirit in which it is offered: as a general orientation, not a final authority.

The goal is not to give you a checklist to follow, but to help you understand how these systems work, what they tend to care about, and what questions you should be asking as you explore your own options. Think of these country profiles as case studies—ways to see patterns across different jurisdictions rather than rules etched in stone.

A few important framing points:

First, entry requirements are always conditional. Visas are permissions, not rights. Even well-documented applications can be delayed or denied. Expect discretion, not guarantees.

Second, most countries are not trying to attract "expats" in the abstract. They are trying to attract specific categories of people: retirees with income, workers with skills, investors with capital, families with stability, or entrepreneurs with potential. Understanding which category you fall into is more important than memorizing forms.

Third, the same rule can feel very different depending on how you approach it. Entry systems reward preparation, patience, and credibility. They punish urgency, entitlement, and improvisation. Many people fail not because the requirements are impossible, but because they underestimate how seriously they are enforced.

Finally, nothing in this appendix replaces professional advice. If you are making a significant move—selling property, relocating family, restructuring finances—you should consult qualified immigration professionals and local counsel. This appendix is meant to make those conversations smarter, not to substitute for them.

Each country profile will outline the general pathways most Americans explore, the typical documentation involved, and the mindset required to navigate the process successfully. Where possible, we highlight common misunderstandings and practical realities—what looks simple on paper but proves complex in practice, and what often matters more than people expect.

Taken together, these ten case studies are meant to do something larger than explain visas. They are meant to show you how states think about entry, residence, and belonging—and how you, as an individual, can engage with those systems realistically and respectfully.

Treat these countries as starting points, not finish lines. Use them to clarify your priorities, sharpen your questions, and understand the tradeoffs inherent in any international move.

Above all, remember this: rules change, but patterns endure. And if you learn how to read the rules, you will always be better prepared—wherever you decide to go next.

CANADA

Opportunity, Innovation, and Quality of Life

Among the countries most frequently considered by Americans looking beyond U.S. borders, Canada occupies a distinctive and often understated position. It is familiar enough to feel accessible, yet structurally different enough to offer a meaningful alternative. Canada combines economic strength with political stability, global connectivity with regional opportunity, and a public philosophy that treats immigration not as an exception, but as a central pillar of national development.

Canada's immigration system is built on an explicit and legally embedded commitment to multiculturalism. This is not merely rhetorical. Immigration targets are published years in advance, policy objectives are publicly articulated, and pathways are designed to align newcomers with long-term economic and demographic needs. For Americans accustomed to a more fragmented and politically volatile immigration environment, this predictability is itself a material advantage.

From a macro perspective, Canada functions as a global hub for education, healthcare, research, and innovation. Its universities and research institutions attract international talent, while its publicly funded healthcare system consistently ranks among the most accessible in the developed world. For professionals, entrepreneurs, and families alike, this translates into a quality of life that extends beyond income alone—encompassing security, mobility, and institutional trust.

Regional Diversity as a Strategic Advantage

One of Canada's defining characteristics is its regional diversity. The country's ten provinces and three territories are not interchangeable: each maintains its own economic profile, labor market priorities, and, in many cases, immigration streams.

Ontario and British Columbia anchor technology, finance, and international business. Quebec offers a distinct cultural and linguistic ecosystem with its own immigration framework. The Prairie provinces emphasize energy, agriculture, and manufacturing. Atlantic Canada focuses on demographic renewal and community-based growth. For applicants willing to look beyond a single city or province, this diversity significantly expands the range of viable entry points.

This decentralized structure means that opportunity in Canada is often geographic. Where an applicant is willing to live can matter as much as credentials, capital, or professional experience.

Investment Climate and Economic Access

For investors and entrepreneurs, Canada presents a compelling balance of stability and access. The political system is predictable, property rights are strong, and the financial sector is tightly regulated but globally integrated. Canada provides access not only to its domestic market, but also to the United States, Europe, and Asia through trade agreements and geographic positioning.

Government policy plays an active role in encouraging innovation and business development. Canada has invested heavily in research and development, clean technology, artificial intelligence, life sciences, and advanced manufacturing. Incentives and programs are designed to attract productive capital—that creates jobs, builds enterprises, and contributes to long-term economic capacity—rather than purely passive investment.

Canada's Immigration Framework

Canada does not offer a single, unified "golden visa" in the traditional sense. Instead, it provides a structured ecosystem of immigration pathways for entrepreneurs, skilled workers, and investors. Successful applicants typically obtain permanent resident (PR) status, which confers the right to live and work anywhere in Canada and access public services, including healthcare. After meeting residency requirements—generally three years of physical presence within five years—permanent residents may apply for citizenship.

Entrepreneur and Innovation Pathways

Historically, Canada has offered dedicated programs for entrepreneurs and active investors. The most prominent has been the Start-up Visa Program, which linked permanent residency to the creation of an innovative, scalable business supported by designated Canadian investors or incubators.

As with all immigration systems, policy evolves. Under changes implemented by Immigration, Refugees and Citizenship Canada, the Start-up Visa Program is closed to new applicants after December 31, 2025. Applicants holding valid 2025 commitment certificates may continue through processing until June 30, 2026, ahead of a new entrepreneur pilot expected to launch in 2026. This shift reflects recalibration rather than retreat, as Canada continues to seek entrepreneurial talent under updated frameworks aligned with current priorities.

Skilled Worker and Provincial Pathways

Canada offers robust migration routes for skilled workers. The federal Express Entry system remains one of the most prominent, operating on a points-based model that evaluates education, work experience, language proficiency, and age. Invitations are competitive and aligned with labor market demand rather than issued on a first-come basis.

Complementing the federal Express Entry system are Provincial Nominee Programs (PNPs), which allow provinces and territories to nominate candidates who meet regional economic needs. These programs often include streams for skilled workers, entrepreneurs, international graduates, and, in some cases, semi-skilled labor. For many applicants, provincial nomination is the decisive factor in securing permanent residency.

Canada also operates region-specific initiatives such as the Atlantic Immigration Program, designed to address labor shortages and population decline in Atlantic provinces. These programs often offer more accessible criteria in exchange for a commitment to settle in designated regions.

Passive Investment: The Quebec Exception

For high-net-worth individuals seeking a more passive investment-based route, Quebec has historically stood apart through the Québec Immigrant Investor Program. This program has required substantial net worth, management experience, and a qualifying investment through a Quebec-based financial intermediary. While subject to periodic pauses and revisions, it illustrates the degree of autonomy provinces retain over immigration policy within the Canadian federation.

Strategic Takeaway

Canada's approach offers a clear lesson for prospective expatriates and investors: opportunity exists, but it is structured. Canada rewards alignment, preparation, and long-term intent. It favors applicants who view immigration not as a transactional purchase, but as a reciprocal relationship—one defined by economic participation, social integration, and geographic flexibility.

Canada demonstrates what a modern, rules-based immigration system looks like when immigration is treated as a strategic asset. For Americans considering relocation, it offers safety, stability, and opportunity—but only for those willing to engage thoughtfully with its requirements and realities.

GREECE

Where History Meets Modern Living

Few countries embody continuity as completely as Greece. Ancient history, Mediterranean geography, and contemporary European life coexist here in a way that feels lived rather than curated. Temples and archaeological ruins stand beside cafés and co-working spaces; island rhythms coexist with EU regulations; deeply rooted, family-centered traditions persist within a modern legal and economic framework. For Americans considering life abroad, Greece offers something increasingly rare: cultural depth paired with practical access to Europe.

Geographically and politically, Greece occupies a strategic position at the crossroads of Europe, the Middle East, and North Africa. At the same time, it is firmly anchored within the European Union and the Schengen Zone. This dual identity makes Greece particularly attractive to internationally mobile residents seeking both lifestyle and access. Visa-free movement across the Schengen Zone, entry to EU markets, and the long-term possibility of European citizenship all factor heavily into Greece's appeal.

Culturally, Greece is known for its openness and hospitality. Social life tends to be relational rather than transactional, and many newcomers find everyday interactions warmer and less formal than in Northern Europe. The cost of living remains comparatively moderate by EU standards, especially outside the most saturated tourist zones. At the same time, infrastructure—healthcare, transportation, telecommunications, and banking—meets modern European expectations, particularly in urban centers and on larger islands.

Greece as a Residency and Investment Gateway

Over the past decade, Greece has deliberately positioned itself as a gateway country for long-term foreign residents. In the wake of financial restructuring, the government moved to attract foreign capital, stabilize the real estate market, and leverage EU membership to bring internationally mobile individuals into the country. The result is a residency framework that appeals to investors, retirees, and location-independent professionals alike.

At the center of this strategy is the Greece Golden Visa, widely regarded as one of Europe's most accessible residency-by-investment programs. Rather than requiring business creation or employment, the program allows non-EU nationals to obtain renewable permanent residence through qualifying investments. Residence permits are issued for five-year periods and may be renewed indefinitely, provided the underlying investment is maintained.

Investment Structure and Compliance

What distinguishes the Greek Golden Visa is its relative flexibility. Qualifying investments include residential real estate purchases, capital contributions to Greek companies or investment funds, and fixed-term deposits with Greek financial institutions. Real estate thresholds vary by location and property type. High-demand areas such as central Athens, Thessaloniki, and certain islands now require higher minimum investments, while other regions remain more accessible.

Special provisions apply to properties converted from commercial to residential use or to historically significant buildings restored by the investor. At the same time, Greece has tightened compliance around property use. Properties acquired under the Golden Visa may not be used for short-term rentals such as Airbnb. Violations can result in fines or revocation of residency, reflecting a broader policy shift toward encouraging long-term residents rather than speculative or purely touristic ownership.

From Residency to Citizenship

The Golden Visa provides more than residency alone. It confers visa-free travel throughout the Schengen Zone and establishes a long-term pathway toward citizenship. After seven years of continuous residency—interpreted in practice as spending the majority of each year in Greece—residents may apply for Greek citizenship, subject to language proficiency and integration requirements.

Citizenship transforms residency into full EU membership, granting the right to live, work, and study across all 27 European Union member states. For many applicants, the Golden Visa functions less as an endpoint than as a strategic bridge toward European citizenship.

Alternative Residency Pathways

Beyond investment-based residency, Greece offers additional pathways that appeal to different profiles. The Digital Nomad Visa allows remote workers employed by non-Greek companies to reside in Greece while maintaining foreign income. For retirees and financially independent individuals, residence permits based on stable, passive income—such as pensions or investment returns—offer another route to long-term residence without local employment.

Greece also stands out for Americans with ancestral ties. Greek citizenship by descent is a powerful and often underappreciated option. Individuals with a Greek parent—and in many cases a Greek grandparent—may be eligible to claim citizenship by documenting each generational link through official records. While administratively demanding, this pathway bypasses residency requirements entirely and grants immediate EU citizenship.

Process, Expectations, and Fit

From a bureaucratic standpoint, Greece illustrates a recurring theme: rules matter, but process matters just as much. Greek administration is formal and document-driven, with an emphasis on certified records, translations, and proof of continuity—particularly in citizenship-by-descent cases. Timelines are rarely

fast, but they are generally predictable when approached methodically and with experienced local professionals.

Greece demonstrates how lifestyle appeal and legal structure can align. It offers sun, sea, history, and community, alongside defined residency pathways, EU mobility, and a credible route to citizenship. For Americans seeking a European base that balances emotional richness with strategic advantage, Greece remains one of the most compelling case studies in modern expatriation.

Like all case studies offered here, Greece should be viewed not as a promise, but as a possibility—one shaped by law, culture, and personal fit. Approached thoughtfully, it offers not just a place to live, but a place to belong.

ITALY

Lifestyle, Culture, and Opportunity

Italy offers Americans a compelling blend of cultural richness and practical opportunity within the European Union. Daily life is shaped by history, food, relationships, and public space, creating a slower, more human rhythm that contrasts with the pace of the United States, while still providing modern infrastructure, high-quality healthcare, reliable internet, and top-ranked universities.

As an EU and Schengen member, Italy provides residents with broad freedom of movement across Europe and, over time, the possibility to live and work anywhere in the EU. Italy has intentionally positioned itself to attract new residents through structured tax incentives and multiple visa pathways for retirees, investors, entrepreneurs, and remote workers, emphasizing genuine residence and integration rather than short-term or transactional stays.

Investors can pursue residency through several routes tied to long-term economic contribution, including startups, company equity, government bonds, or philanthropic investments. Financially independent individuals often favor the

Elective Residency Visa, which allows long-term residence without employment, provided applicants can demonstrate stable passive income and commit to living in Italy year-round. This pathway can lead to permanent residency after five years and citizenship after ten, with Italy permitting dual citizenship.

Italy has also adapted to modern work patterns through its Digital Nomad and Remote Worker Visa, enabling highly skilled professionals to live in Italy while working for foreign employers or clients. These permits are renewable and can lead to permanent residence, making Italy viable not just for retirees but also for globally mobile professionals and families.

Families benefit from access to Italy's public healthcare system, public education, and strong higher-education institutions, with family reunification available under most long-term permits. While Italian bureaucracy is formal, document-intensive, and sometimes slow, it is generally predictable when handled carefully, rewarding preparation, patience, and respect for process.

Overall, Italy exemplifies a central theme of expatriation: lifestyle and legality must align. It offers extraordinary cultural depth and quality of life, but expects real commitment, compliance, and integration in return. For Americans seeking balance, continuity, and long-term European opportunity, Italy remains one of the most enduring and attractive choices.

MALTA

Navigating Business & Lifestyle Opportunities in the Mediterranean

Malta occupies a distinctive position in Europe: small in geography, but outsized in institutional reach. With layers of history spanning millennia, a strategic location at the crossroads of Europe, North Africa, and the Middle East, and a modern, internationally-oriented economy, Malta has emerged as one of Europe's most functional destinations for globally mobile individuals.

What draws people to Malta is not a single advantage, but a carefully balanced system. English is an official language; the legal framework blends British common law traditions with European Union regulation; and the financial sector is sophisticated, well-capitalized, and closely supervised. At the same time, daily life unfolds against a Mediterranean backdrop of coastline, walkable historic cities, and a pace of life that appeals equally to retirees, entrepreneurs, and remote professionals.

As a full member of the European Union and the Schengen Area, Malta offers residents visa-free travel across much of Europe, while retaining a legal and administrative culture that is unusually accessible to English-speaking Americans.

A Modular Residency Framework

From a residency and planning perspective, Malta stands out for the range of structured options it offers. Rather than a one-size-fits-all model, Malta has developed distinct programs tailored to investors, high-net-worth individuals, retirees, and digital nomads. This modular approach allows individuals to select a pathway aligned with how they actually live, earn, and move internationally.

Malta Permanent Residence Programme (MPRP)

One of Malta's most prominent offerings is the Malta Permanent Residence Programme. This residency-by-investment framework allows non-EU nationals to obtain permanent residence through a three-part commitment: qualifying real estate (purchase or long-term rental), a government contribution, and a registered charitable donation.

Unlike many residency programs, the MPRP does not impose a physical residence requirement to maintain status. This feature makes it particularly attractive to internationally mobile families who want EU residency and long-term legal stability without relocating full-time. The program is also notable for its expansive family definition, which can include spouses, dependent children up to age 29, parents, grandparents, and—under certain conditions—future generations.

Permanent residents under the MPRP enjoy visa-free travel throughout the Schengen Zone for short stays and access to Malta's infrastructure and services. Importantly, the program is designed to provide permanence without political integration; it is not a direct or accelerated pathway to citizenship.

Tax-Oriented Residency: The Global Residence Programme

For individuals prioritizing tax efficiency alongside residency, the Malta Global Residence Programme is often the most compelling option. The GRP grants a special tax status to qualifying non-EU/EEA nationals, applying a flat 15% tax rate on foreign income remitted to Malta, subject to a minimum annual tax.

Foreign income not remitted to Malta is not taxed, and foreign capital gains remain exempt even if brought into the country. Malta imposes no wealth tax, no inheritance tax, and no property tax, while also offering access to extensive double-taxation treaties. This framework makes Malta particularly attractive to investors, retirees, and business owners with diversified international income streams.

The GRP is designed for flexibility. There is no minimum stay requirement, allowing residents to maintain Maltese residency while spending substantial time elsewhere. Applicants must acquire qualifying property, demonstrate financial self-sufficiency, maintain comprehensive health insurance, and pass rigorous due-diligence checks. Family members may be included and benefit from access to Malta's healthcare and education systems.

Digital Nomads and Retirees

Malta has also adapted to modern work patterns through the Malta Nomad Residence Permit, which allows remote workers to live in Malta while working for employers or clients based abroad. For professionals seeking EU access without severing foreign employment ties, Malta offers a rare combination of lifestyle appeal, English-language administration, and legal clarity.

For retirees, the Malta Retirement Programme provides a tailored solution for individuals with stable retirement income. As with other Maltese programs, it emphasizes financial independence, compliance, and long-term stability rather than employment or active investment.

Tax Structure, Compliance, and Reality

Across all residency programs, Malta's tax framework is a central attraction. Remittance-based taxation, the absence of wealth and inheritance taxes, and predictable rules create a planning environment well-suited to high-net-worth

individuals. At the same time, Malta enforces strict due diligence. Background checks are thorough, financial records are scrutinized, and ongoing compliance is mandatory.

There are important caveats. Programs such as the Global Residence Programme do not provide guaranteed or accelerated citizenship. While Maltese law allows naturalization after extended periods of lawful residence, approvals generally require deep and sustained integration and are not automatic. Annual tax filings, property compliance, and reporting obligations are non-negotiable, and failure to comply can jeopardize residency status.

Strategic Takeaway

Malta illustrates a central lesson for globally mobile Americans: residency, taxation, and lifestyle can be aligned—but only through careful planning. Malta rewards clarity of intent, transparency of finances, and respect for process. In return, it offers exceptional flexibility, EU access, and a high quality of life in one of Europe's safest and most internationally connected jurisdictions.

For those seeking a Mediterranean base that accommodates business, travel, family, and long-term planning, Malta remains one of Europe's most deliberately designed residency destinations—not flashy, but deeply functional, and increasingly relevant in a mobile world.

PANAMA

The Crossroads of the Americas

Panama occupies a uniquely strategic position at the geographic intersection of North and South America. This narrow isthmus has shaped global trade for centuries and continues to play a central role in international commerce. Its tropical climate and extraordinary biodiversity coexist with a modern, service-oriented economy that has experienced sustained growth over the past two decades.

Culturally, Panama reflects a complex blending of Indigenous, European, and African influences. Its population, institutions, and business practices mirror this diversity, contributing to a society that is outward-facing and internationally engaged. Panama's importance to the global economy is anchored by the Panama Canal, a critical artery of maritime trade linking the Atlantic and Pacific oceans.

From a financial perspective, Panama's use of the U.S. dollar as legal tender provides monetary stability, reduces currency risk, and simplifies cross-border transactions for foreign investors. Combines with a territorial tax system that generally exempts foreign-sourced income from local taxation, these features have made Panama a long-standing hub for international banking, logistics, and professional services.

Panama Qualified Investor Visa

The Panama Qualified Investor Visa—often referred to as a golden visa in other jurisdictions—grants permanent residency to foreign nationals who make a qualifying investment in the country. The program is part of Panama's broader strategy to attract foreign capital, promote economic development, and reinforce its position as a regional financial and commercial center.

This residency pathway provides immediate permanent resident status and allows successful applicants to live, work, and study in Panama. It also offers access to the local banking system, facilitates international mobility, and provides long-term optionality for individuals seeking geographic diversification.

Applications may be completed remotely and are processed through licensed Panamanian attorneys. Approvals are commonly issued in approximately 30 days, making the program one of the more administratively efficient residency-by-investment options available. Eligible family members may be included in the application alongside the primary applicant.

Qualifying Investment Options

Panama's residency-by-investment framework is best understood not as a relocation mandate, but as a long-term strategic option—providing legal residency, financial access, and future mobility in a stable, dollar-based jurisdiction at the center of global trade.

To qualify under the Panama Qualified Investor Visa, applicants must make one of the following investments:

- Real Estate Investment

A minimum investment of US $300,000 in Panamanian property. Ownership may be held directly in the applicant's name, through a trust, or via a legal entity.

- Securities Investment

A minimum investment of US $500,000 in securities registered with Panama's Securities Market Superintendency and held through a licensed brokerage firm.

- Bank Deposit

A minimum deposit of US $750,000 in an approved Panamanian bank, held free of encumbrances for a period of five years.

All qualifying investments must be maintained for at least five years in order to preserve residency status and future eligibility for citizenship.

Residency and Citizenship Timeline

Month 1 — Application Preparation and Submission

The applicant selects an investment route, completes the qualifying investment, and assembles required documentation. The application is submitted through a licensed Panamanian attorney.

Month 2 — Approval and Permanent Residency

Processing typically takes approximately 30 days. Upon approval, permanent residency is granted. The applicant must visit Panama within two years to provide biometrics and receive a permanent residency card.

Ongoing — Residency Maintenance

Permanent residents must visit Panama at least once every two years and maintain their qualifying investment for a minimum of five years.

Month 60 — Eligibility for Citizenship

After five years of permanent residency, applicants become eligible to apply for Panamanian citizenship, subject to additional requirements, including language and civic knowledge examinations.

Month 61–72 — Citizenship Approval

Citizenship applications are reviewed by multiple government entities. Final approval typically occurs within six to twelve months and is formalized through a presidential decree of naturalization.

PORTUGAL

Old-World Charm, Modern Opportunity

Situated at the western edge of the Iberian Peninsula, Portugal combines deep historical continuity with a modern European framework. Long shaped by maritime exploration and global exchange, the country today offers a laid-back Mediterranean lifestyle, a rich and diverse culture, and a legal and institutional environment firmly anchored within the European Union.

Geographically, Portugal presents remarkable variety within a relatively compact territory. The sunlit beaches and cliffs of the Algarve contrast with the vineyard-lined Douro Valley and the cooler, mountainous regions of the north. Historic cities such as Lisbon and Porto retain their architectural character while supporting contemporary infrastructure, international business activity, and growing technology and creative sectors. This coexistence of old-world charm and modern development is central to Portugal's appeal.

As a member of the European Union and the Schengen Area, Portugal provides residents with visa-free travel across much of Europe, access to EU markets, and long-term regulatory stability—key considerations for individuals planning multi-year or multi-generational relocations.

Portugal Residency by Investment

Portugal has been widely recognized for its residency-by-investment framework, commonly referred to as the Portugal Golden Visa. While the program has evolved, its core structure reflects Portugal's broader approach to immigration: encouraging long-term engagement rather than short-term speculation.

Under current rules, residency may be obtained through qualifying investments aligned with national priorities. One of the most prominent routes involves a minimum qualifying contribution of €250,000, typically directed toward approved cultural, artistic, or heritage-preservation initiatives. Other investment routes, often at higher thresholds, may include regulated investment funds or business activity.

Successful applicants and their immediate family members are granted renewable residence permits with the right to live, work, and study in Portugal. The program requires only limited physical presence, making it compatible with internationally mobile lifestyles. After five years of legal residency, applicants may seek permanent residence or Portuguese citizenship, subject to language and integration requirements.

Employment- and Activity-Based Residency Options

Portugal also offers a broad set of non-investment residency pathways tailored to different professional and income profiles. Together, these pathways illustrate Portugal's flexible and segmented approach to residency, allowing applicants to select routes aligned with how they live and earn rather than forcing uniform criteria.

D1 Work Visa–
Designed for non-EU nationals who have accepted a job offer from a Portuguese employer, allowing them to live, work, and study in Portugal.

D2 Entrepreneur Visa–
Intended for entrepreneurs, business owners, and self-employed professionals who wish to establish or operate a business in Portugal, including freelancers working under self-employment arrangements with Portuguese entities.

Highly Qualified Activity Visa–
A long-term residency option aimed at attracting highly skilled professionals, including executives, senior managers, engineers, scientists, healthcare professionals, legal specialists, and senior public-sector or corporate officers.

D7 Passive Income Visa–
Designed for retirees and financially independent individuals with stable passive income, such as pensions or investment income. The initial residence permit is typically valid for two years, renewable for three years, with eligibility for permanent residence and citizenship after five years. Limited professional activity is permitted.

Digital Nomad Visa–
Allows remote workers and freelancers employed by non-Portuguese companies to live in Portugal while maintaining foreign income sources, reflecting Portugal's adaptation to modern work patterns.

Citizenship and the Portuguese Passport

Portuguese citizenship may be acquired through birth, descent, marriage, or naturalization. For most foreign residents, naturalization requires five years of legal residency, along with basic Portuguese language proficiency and proof of integration. Once citizenship is granted, individuals may apply for a Portuguese passport.

Portugal's passport is widely regarded as one of the stronger travel documents globally. Portuguese citizens enjoy visa-free or visa-on-arrival access to a large number of destinations worldwide, along with full rights to live, work, and study across the European Union. EU citizenship also provides access to public healthcare, education, and labor markets throughout the bloc.

Beyond mobility, Portuguese citizenship offers long-term security and continuity. Citizenship can be passed to future generations, transforming an individual residency decision into a lasting family asset.

Process, Compliance, and Reality

Portugal's administrative system is formal and document-driven. Residency and citizenship applications emphasize compliance, continuity, and recordkeeping rather than speed. Timelines can vary, but outcomes are generally predictable when applications are prepared carefully and supported by qualified local professionals.

As with all jurisdictions discussed in here, Portugal's programs are governed by evolving legislation and administrative practice. Investment thresholds, eligible routes, and procedural requirements may change, underscoring the importance of up-to-date planning and realistic expectations.

Strategic Takeaway

Portugal demonstrates how lifestyle appeal and legal structure can align within a stable European framework. It offers climate, culture, and community alongside EU access, defined residency pathways, and a clear route to citizenship.

For Americans seeking a European base that balances quality of life with long-term legal clarity and global mobility, Portugal remains one of the most balanced and durable case studies in modern expatriation—quietly functional, institutionally sound, and deeply livable.

SPAIN

Lifestyle, Culture, and Opportunity

Spain is the largest country in Southern Europe and the fourth most populous member of the European Union. Long shaped by imperial history, regional diversity, and Mediterranean geography, Spain offers a combination of cultural depth, modern infrastructure, and institutional stability that continues to attract international residents from across the globe.

Spain is defined by variety. Coastal regions along the Mediterranean and Atlantic offer mild climates and beach-oriented living, while interior cities and northern regions provide cooler weather, strong regional identities, and thriving urban economies. Major metropolitan centers such as Madrid, Barcelona, and Valencia support international business, education, and technology, while smaller cities and towns offer a slower pace at significantly lower cost.

Spain's public systems are a central part of its appeal. The country maintains a strong, widely accessible healthcare system and a well-developed education sector, including public universities and internationally-recognized private institutions. Compared with many other Western European countries, Spain's cost of living remains relatively low—particularly in housing, food, transportation, and healthcare—making it attractive to retirees, families, and location-independent professionals alike.

As a member of the European Union and the Schengen Area, Spain provides residents with visa-free travel across much of Europe and access to EU markets and legal protections. For Americans considering long-term relocation, this combination of lifestyle and structural access is a significant draw.

Citizenship by Ancestry: Democratic Memory Law

Spain offered at one time a notable citizenship pathway for individuals with Spanish ancestry through its Citizenship by Democratic Memory Law. This law allowed descendants of Spaniards who left the country due to exile during the Spanish Civil War and subsequent dictatorship to apply for Spanish citizenship.

Eligibility extended to children, grandchildren, and—under limited circumstances—great-grandchildren of affected Spaniards. However, this pathway was time-limited. The deadline for grandchildren and great-grandchildren to submit applications was 22 October 2025, and no new applications are accepted after that date. While this route has now closed, it remains an important example of how Spain has used citizenship policy to address historical displacement and diaspora ties.

Residency Pathways for Non-EU Nationals

Spain does not operate a single, unified residency framework. Instead, it offers a range of visas tailored to different income sources, employment structures, and life stages.

Non-Lucrative (Retirement) Visa–

The Spain Non-Lucrative Visa, often referred to as the Retirement Visa, allows non-EU nationals to reside in Spain without engaging in employment. Applicants must demonstrate sufficient passive income—such as pensions, investment income, rental income, or savings—and agree not to work in Spain or abroad during the visa's validity.

This visa is particularly popular among retirees and financially independent individuals seeking long-term residence in Spain. While employment is prohibited, the visa provides a clear pathway to permanent residency and eventual citizenship after meeting residency requirements.

Digital Nomad Visa–

Spain's Digital Nomad Visa reflects the country's adaptation to modern work patterns. It allows non-EU/EEA nationals to live in Spain while working remotely for employers or clients based outside Spain. The visa is available to both salaried employees and freelancers or contractors, provided the majority of income is generated from non-Spanish sources.

This pathway appeals to professionals seeking EU residence without severing foreign employment relationships and combines legal clarity with Spain's lifestyle advantages.

Highly Qualified Professional Visa–

The Highly Qualified Professional Visa is designed for skilled foreign workers with a university degree or substantial professional experience. It targets roles in sectors such as technology, engineering, healthcare, research, and senior management. Sponsorship by a Spanish employer is typically required, and the visa offers a streamlined route for experienced professionals entering Spain's labor market.

Self-Employed Visa–

The Self-Employed Visa allows non-EU nationals to live in Spain while operating their own business or working as freelancers. Applicants must present a viable business plan, demonstrate relevant qualifications or experience, and show sufficient financial resources. This visa is often used by entrepreneurs, consultants, and independent professionals seeking long-term establishment in Spain.

From Residency to Citizenship

Spain allows foreign residents to apply for citizenship after ten years of legal residence, with reduced timelines available for certain nationalities and circumstances. Citizenship grants full EU rights, including the ability to live, work, and study throughout the European Union, as well as visa-free or visa-on-arrival access to a wide range of countries worldwide.

Spanish citizenship is particularly valuable for individuals seeking long-term European integration, though the path requires sustained residence, language proficiency, and cultural integration.

Process, Compliance, and Fit

Spain's administrative system is formal and documentation-driven. Residency applications require careful preparation, proof of financial capacity, and adherence to specific visa conditions. Timelines can vary by region and consulate, but outcomes are generally predictable when applications are structured correctly and supported by experienced local professionals.

Spain should be approached as a long-term legal and lifestyle decision rather than a transactional move. Visa conditions matter, compliance is ongoing, and residency choices should align with how applicants intend to live and earn.

Strategic Takeaway

Spain illustrates how lifestyle appeal, cultural richness, and institutional access can converge. It offers climate, cuisine, community, and affordability alongside EU membership, modern infrastructure, and multiple residency pathways.

For Americans seeking a European base that balances quality of life with long-term opportunity—whether through retirement, remote work, professional engagement, or entrepreneurship—Spain remains one of the most versatile and accessible options in modern expatriation.

SWITZERLAND

A Safe Haven in Europe

Switzerland occupies a singular position in Europe. Long associated with political neutrality, financial sophistication, and institutional reliability, it has become one of the continent's most stable destinations for globally mobile individuals and families. While not a member of the European Union, Switzerland is deeply integrated into the European and global economy and consistently ranks among the safest countries in the world.

From a quality-of-life perspective, Switzerland sets an unusually high bar. Cities are clean, orderly, and secure. Infrastructure functions with precision. Public transportation is efficient and comprehensive, healthcare and education systems are world-class, and environmental quality—from alpine air to pristine lakes—is tightly protected. For Americans considering relocation, Switzerland often represents not change for its own sake, but continuity: a place where systems work predictably and long-term planning is feasible.

Geographically, Switzerland sits at the heart of Europe, bordering major EU economies while maintaining its own sovereign framework. It participates in the Schengen Area, enabling visa-free travel across much of Europe, and functions as a natural hub for international business, diplomacy, and wealth management.

Economic Stability and Business Environment

Switzerland's reputation as a safe haven is rooted in its economic structure. The country combines a strong currency, disciplined fiscal policy, and an exceptionally stable banking system. Core industries include banking and finance, pharmaceuticals, precision manufacturing, technology, and advanced research. Intellectual property protection is robust, contracts are reliably enforced, and regulatory frameworks are clear and consistent.

For investors and entrepreneurs, Switzerland offers a business-friendly environment with competitive tax regimes at the cantonal level, political predictability, and deep capital markets. While the cost of living is high by European standards, it is matched by commensurate income levels, services, and institutional quality.

Switzerland's passport is consistently ranked among the most powerful globally, providing extensive visa-free or visa-on-arrival access worldwide and reinforcing the country's role as a base for internationally active individuals.

Lifestyle, Culture, and Social Framework

Swiss society places a premium on privacy, order, and reliability. The culture is calm, efficient, and pragmatic, shaped by federalism and local autonomy. With four national languages—German, French, Italian, and Romansh—Switzerland reflects a multicultural identity within a highly structured civic framework.

Daily life is organized and predictable. Public transport runs on schedule, public services are efficient, and civic trust is high. For families, Switzerland offers safety, excellent schooling options (including international schools), and access to top-tier healthcare. For individuals seeking discretion and long-term stability, the country's emphasis on privacy remains a major draw.

Residency and Expenditure-Based (Lump-Sum) Taxation

One of Switzerland's most distinctive features for high-net-worth individuals is its lump-sum taxation regime, formally known as expenditure-based taxation. Rather than taxing worldwide income and assets directly, this system calculates taxable income based on an individual's annual living expenses in Switzerland.

The tax base is determined through a control calculation to ensure it is not lower than the tax that would be payable on Swiss-source income and assets. This framework is administered under the oversight of the Swiss Federal Tax Administration and implemented at the cantonal level, where conditions and acceptance may vary.

Under current rules, the taxable amount must be at least the highest of the following benchmarks:

- CHF 434,700 (federal minimum for 2025, adjusted periodically)
- Seven times the annual rent or rental value of the primary Swiss residence
- Three times the annual cost of full board and lodging if residing in a hotel or similar accommodation
- Total Swiss-source income, including income from Swiss real estate, movable assets, intellectual property rights, pensions, rents, annuities, or income subject to a double taxation agreement

This regime is typically available only to foreign nationals who do not engage in gainful employment in Switzerland. Acceptance is discretionary and subject to negotiation with cantonal authorities, as well as comprehensive due diligence.

Strategic Takeaway

Switzerland illustrates what institutional excellence looks like when stability, privacy, and economic strength are treated as core national assets. It does not compete on affordability or speed of entry; rather, it appeals to individuals and families seeking security, discretion, and long-term reliability within one of the world's most trusted jurisdictions.

For Americans prioritizing safety, refined living standards, and a business environment where rules are clear and consistently enforced, Switzerland remains a benchmark destination in Europe—not aspirational in tone, but foundational in function.

TURKEY

Where Continents and Opportunities Meet

Turkey occupies one of the world's most strategic geographic positions, bridging Europe, Asia, and the Middle East. This crossroads location has shaped the country's history as a center of trade, culture, and diplomacy—and continues to define its modern role as a regional economic hub. For internationally mobile individuals, Turkey offers a rare combination of scale, affordability, and access to multiple markets.

From a lifestyle perspective, Turkey is strikingly diverse. Global cities such as Istanbul operate as financial, cultural, and transportation centers, while coastal regions along the Mediterranean and Aegean offer resort-style living, mild climates, and a comparatively low cost of living. Inland regions provide historic towns, agricultural wealth, and growing industrial zones. This breadth allows residents to align lifestyle choices with professional or investment goals rather than being constrained to a single urban model.

Turkey's healthcare system is universal and modern, with both public and private options widely available. Education is another draw, with a growing number of internationally accredited universities and private schools—particularly appealing to families considering long-term residence or citizenship.

Why Turkey Attracts Global Investors

Turkey's appeal rests on accessibility and value. The cost of living is significantly lower than in most Western European countries, while infrastructure—airports, highways, telecommunications, and healthcare—has seen substantial investment over the past two decades. Combined with an expat-friendly environment and a dynamic real estate market, this has positioned Turkey as one of the most active citizenship-by-investment destinations globally.

Politically and economically, Turkey functions as a bridge economy. Investors gain exposure to both European and Asian markets, supported by a large domestic population and diversified industries ranging from manufacturing and tourism to technology and finance.

Turkish Citizenship by Investment

At the center of Turkey's international mobility strategy is the Turkey Citizenship by Investment Program, sometimes referred to as the Turkey Golden Visa. This program allows foreign nationals to obtain full Turkish citizenship by making a qualifying investment in the country's economy.

The most commonly used pathway is real estate investment, requiring a minimum purchase of USD $400,000, held for at least three years. Investors may acquire a single property or multiple properties to meet the threshold, and there is no requirement to occupy the property.

Alternative qualifying investments include:

- USD $500,000 bank deposit held for three years
- USD $500,000 in government bonds
- USD $500,000 capital investment in a Turkish business
- USD $500,000 investment fund share (real estate or venture capital)
- Creation of 50 full-time jobs

Once the investment is completed, applicants may submit their citizenship application. Processing typically results in citizenship approval within 6 to 12 months, making it one of the faster citizenship-by-investment programs globally.

Benefits of Turkish Citizenship

Turkish citizenship confers full nationality rights, including the issuance of a Turkish passport. Key benefits include:

- Visa-free or facilitated travel to over 120 countries worldwide
- No minimum residency requirement and no language testing
- Eligibility for the U.S. E-2 Treaty Investor Visa, as Turkey is an E-2 treaty country with the United States
- Family inclusion, allowing spouses and dependent children under 18 (and dependent adult children with disabilities) to be included
- Dual citizenship permitted, allowing investors to retain existing nationalities
- Access to Turkey's healthcare and education systems
- Requirements and Compliance

To qualify, the primary applicant must:

- Be at least 18 years old
- Hold a clean criminal record
- Maintain adequate health insurance
- Have no history of illegal overstay in Turkey
- Meet nationality eligibility requirements

Certain nationalities are excluded from the program under Turkish regulations, including Armenia, Cuba, Nigeria, North Korea, and Syria.

Turkey enforces formal due diligence. Documentation, source-of-funds verification, and compliance with holding periods are essential to maintaining citizenship eligibility.

Strategic Takeaway

Turkey illustrates how geography, affordability, and legal structure can converge into a powerful mobility tool. It offers a fast route to citizenship, access to multiple regions, and lifestyle flexibility that few countries can match at a comparable cost.

For Americans seeking a second passport that prioritizes speed, optionality, and value—while retaining access to both Europe and Asia—Turkey remains one of the most pragmatic and strategically useful case studies in modern citizenship planning.

UNITED KINGDOM

A Global Leader in Economy and Opportunity

The United Kingdom occupies a distinctive position in the global economic system. With one of the world's largest and most sophisticated economies, it has long functioned as a center for finance, law, education, innovation, and international trade. For Americans considering relocation, the UK offers institutional depth, cultural familiarity, and access to one of the most globally connected markets.

Although the UK formally exited the European Union, its geographic proximity to the European continent continues to support strong trade, business, and tourism ties. London remains a leading global financial hub, while regional cities such as Manchester, Birmingham, Edinburgh, and Cambridge anchor technology, research, manufacturing, and higher education ecosystems. The result is an economy that is diversified, resilient, and internationally oriented.

Why Choose the United Kingdom?

The UK combines historical continuity with modern economic dynamism. Its multicultural society, long-standing legal traditions, and global influence make it a central player in Europe despite its non-EU status. English is the primary language of government, business, and education, reducing friction for American migrants and easing professional integration.

Public institutions are a major draw. The National Health Service provides universal healthcare access, while the education system includes some of the world's most prestigious universities and research institutions. Infrastructure—transportation, telecommunications, and financial services—is mature and reliable.

While immigration policy has tightened in recent years, the UK continues to actively court highly skilled professionals, entrepreneurs, and innovators through targeted visa categories. The emphasis is less on passive residency and more on contribution, talent, and economic participation.

Innovation, Talent, and Business Visas

Innovator Founder Visa–

The Innovator Founder Visa is designed for entrepreneurs seeking to establish a business in the UK. It replaces earlier startup frameworks and focuses on ventures that are innovative, viable, and scalable. Applicants must demonstrate that they have developed—or played a key role in developing—the underlying business idea, which must be endorsed by an approved UK body.

Unlike traditional investor visas, the Innovator Founder route does not require a fixed minimum investment amount. Instead, it evaluates the quality and growth potential of the proposed business. This visa offers a pathway to permanent residence, typically after three years, provided business milestones are met.

Global Talent Visa–

The Global Talent Visa targets established and emerging leaders in fields such as science, engineering, medicine, technology, arts, and academia. Applicants must receive endorsement from a recognized UK body relevant to their field.

This visa offers exceptional flexibility. There is no minimum investment requirement, no mandatory job offer, and significant freedom to change employers or pursue independent work. The visa is renewable and provides a fast-track route to permanent residency—often after as little as three years—making it one of the UK's most attractive options for highly skilled individuals.

Citizenship by Descent–

The United Kingdom also offers citizenship pathways based on ancestry. British citizenship by descent is typically passed down one generation through a British citizen parent. In some cases, citizenship may also be available through a British grandparent under specific "double descent" provisions, depending on the circumstances of birth, registration, and historical nationality law.

Eligibility criteria vary and can be complex, often requiring careful documentation of lineage, birth records, and citizenship status across generations. When successful, citizenship by descent provides full British nationality rights, including the right to live and work in the UK and access public services.

From Residency to Citizenship

For most migrants, long-term settlement in the UK follows a structured progression. Temporary visas—such as the Innovator Founder or Global Talent visas—can lead to indefinite leave to remain (ILR) after meeting residence and compliance requirements. Once ILR is granted, applicants may apply for British citizenship after an additional qualifying period, subject to language, residency, and good-character requirements.

British citizenship provides a powerful passport, broad global mobility, and long-term legal security in one of the world's most influential countries.

Process, Expectations, and Fit

UK immigration is rules-based and document-intensive. Applications are assessed against clearly defined criteria, and compliance with visa conditions is closely monitored. While the system can feel formal, outcomes are generally predictable when applications are prepared carefully and aligned with policy objectives.

The UK is best approached as a long-term strategic decision rather than a short-term lifestyle experiment. It rewards talent, innovation, and sustained engagement rather than passive presence.

Strategic Takeaway

The United Kingdom illustrates how economic scale, institutional strength, and targeted immigration policy can coexist outside the EU framework. It offers global connectivity, professional opportunity, and cultural familiarity—tempered by higher costs and more rigorous entry requirements.

For Americans seeking a destination that prioritizes career advancement, entrepreneurship, education, and long-term institutional stability, the UK remains one of the most consequential and opportunity-rich relocation options in Europe and beyond.

Navigating a Moving Landscape

The countries examined here illustrate a central reality of modern mobility: there is no single "best" destination—only options that fit particular lives, goals, and timelines. Each jurisdiction offers a different balance of lifestyle, legal structure, tax treatment, residency pathways, and long-term opportunity. What works exceptionally well for a retiree with passive income may be ill-suited to an entrepreneur, a remote professional, or a family planning for future generations.

A second theme runs through every case study: immigration, residency, and citizenship rules change constantly. Investment thresholds rise or fall. Visa categories open, pause, or close. Compliance standards tighten. Political priorities shift. Programs that once appeared permanent can be restructured with little notice, while new pathways may emerge quietly in response to labor shortages, demographic pressures, or economic strategy.

For that reason, this appendix should be read as a strategic framework, not a checklist or promise. It is designed to help readers understand how different countries think about migration—what they reward, what they restrict, and what they expect in return—not serve as definitive legal guidance.

Readers considering action should take one of two prudent next steps:

- Consult a specialized international mobility advisory firm, such as Global Citizen Solutions, that actively monitors program changes and works with licensed local professionals. Firms operating in this space can help translate broad policy into current, country-specific realities and identify pathways aligned with individual circumstances.

- Conduct independent, primary-source research by reviewing official government immigration and interior ministry websites on a country-by-country basis. These sources provide the most authoritative and up-to-date information on eligibility, timelines, documentation requirements, and legal obligations.

Ultimately, successful relocation, residency planning, or citizenship acquisition depends less on finding a "perfect" program than on aligning intent, eligibility, and timing within a rules-based system. Approached thoughtfully—and with current information—international mobility can be not only achievable, but transformative.

About the Author

Scott A. Schwartz is an investment advisor and financial analyst with more than three decades of experience advising cross-border clients. He holds an undergraduate degree in geography, with an emphasis on weather and climate; a master's degree in business with a concentration in finance; and a Master of Liberal Arts degree focused on early modern Europe.

In addition to his professional and academic work in finance and history, Scott has maintained a parallel career as an airline pilot and is an avid global traveler. His lifelong interest in weather, climate, and geography informs both his investment perspective and his writing.

Scott is a Certified Financial Planner™ (CFP®), Certified Investment Management Analyst® (CIMA®), and Accredited Investment Fiduciary® (AIF®). He currently serves as a Principal at International Asset Management Advisors in San Mateo, California.

He is the author of *Investing in a New Climate: A Sustainable Approach to Investing and Living in a New Climate* (2021). His forthcoming book, to be published in 2026, examines water insecurity in early modern Malta under the Knights of St. John.

He divides his time between the San Francisco Bay Area and Malta.

Acknowledgments

I would like to thank my adult children, Jessica and Danielle, for their unwavering intellectual and moral support throughout this project.

Brooke King has been an exceptional editor, helping to shape the manuscript and keep me on track to completion. I am also grateful to Tom Zachystal for sharing his expertise in cross-border consulting, which greatly informed this work.

Special thanks to Jill Turney for her valuable assistance with graphics and layout.

Chapter opener photo credits:

Chapter 1: Christopher Moswitzer | Dreamstime
Chapter 2: © DKosig | iStock
Chapter 3: © Querbeet | iStock
Chapter 4: © Richard Villalor | iStock
Chapter 5: © Ivar Østby Simonsen | iStock
Chapter 6: © AscentXMedia | iStock
Chapter 7: © ilbusca | iStock
Chapter 8: © Alexandrumagurean | iStock
Chapter 9: © Shah Rukh | Dreamstime
Chapter 10: © Naropano | Dreamstime
Chapter 11: © Mikael Damkier | Dreamstime
Chapter 12: © bluecinema | iStock
Chapter 13: © Fabian Plockl | Dreamstime

Appendix photo credits:

CANADA: page 168 © Sean Xu, page 171 © Sean Pavone | iStock
GREECE: page 172 © George Clerk, page 175 © Neirfy | iStock
ITALY: page 176 © Fani Kurti, page 177 © Simon Skafar | iStock
MALTA: page 178 © Alina Zienowicz, page 181 © arcady_31 | iStock
PANAMA: page 182 © SL_Photography, page 185 © Roc Llimargas Llop - a9 photography | iStock
PORTUGAL: page 186 Sean 3810, page 189 © Mercedes Rancaño Otero© Andranik Hakobyan | iStock
SPAIN: page 190 © Rudy Balasko, page 193 © amoklv
SWITZERLAND: page 194 and page 197 © Sean Pavone | iStock
TURKEY: page 198 © Thankful Photography, page 201 © Zzvet | iStock
UNITED KINGDOM: page 202 © John Kellerman, page 205 © Lana 2011 | iStock

Made in United States
Orlando, FL
05 November 2026

90200954R10126